MARCO ⊕ POLO

Travel with **Insider Tips**

VIENNA

Berlin
GERMANY
POLAND
Dresden
Frankfurt
CZECH REPUBLIC
SLOVAKIA
Passau
Munich
Salzburg · **Vienna**
LI
CH
AUSTRIA
HUNGARY
ITALY
SLOVENIA
CROATIA

D0416622

www.marco-polo.com

← INSIDE FRONT COVER: THE BEST HIGHLIGHTS

The best Insider Tips → p. 4

Best of ... → p. 6

Sightseeing → p. 26

Food & Drink → p. 62

SYMBOLS

- INSIDER TIP — Insider Tip
- ★ — Highlight
- ●●●● — Best of ...
- Scenic view
- Responsible travel: fair trade principles and the environment respected

PRICE CATEGORIES HOTELS

Expensive	over 150 euros
Moderate	100–150 euros
Budget	under 100 euros

The prices are for two in a double room per night including breakfast

PRICE CATEGORIES RESTAURANTS

Expensive	over 16 euros
Moderate	10–16 euros
Budget	under 10 euros

The prices are for a main course without drinks and are often considerably lower at lunchtime

On the cover: MuseumsQuartier: a mass of cultural highlights p. 48 | Beach bars on the Danube Canal p. 39

CONTENTS

Shopping → p. 72

Entertainment → p. 80

Where to stay → p. 90

Street atlas → p. 124

DID YOU KNOW?

Relax & Enjoy → p. 39
Keep fit! → p. 43
Green-and-white or violet → p. 47
Books & Films → p. 58
Gourmet restaurants → p. 66
Local specialities → p. 68
Luxury hotels → p. 94
Budgeting → p. 113
Voices of gold → p. 114
Currency converter → p. 116
Weather in Vienna → p. 117

MAPS IN THE GUIDEBOOK

(126 A1) Page numbers and coordinates refer to the street atlas
Map of surrounding area on p. 142/143
(0) Site/address located off the map. Coordinates are also given for places that are not marked on the street atlas.
A public transportation map can be found inside the back cover

INSIDE BACK COVER: PULL-OUT MAP →

PULL-OUT MAP 〰

(〰 A–B 2–3) Refers to the removable pull-out map

The best MARCO POLO Insider Tips

Our top 15 Insider Tips

INSIDER TIP Main music drag

The 'Gürtel' was neglected for a long time but, more recently, it has been revitalised to become a suburban boulevard with a real purpose. Now, many mind-blowing locations – such as *B72* and *Chelsea* – draw in the night owls with their live gigs → **p. 47, 82**

INSIDER TIP Peering into the city's 'cleavage'

The reward for struggling up the 343 steps to the keeper's room in the southern tower of St Stephen's Cathedral is the wonderful view of the labyrinth of streets and sea of houses in the heart of the city (photo above) → **p. 46**

INSIDER TIP Grand opera, free of charge

Mozart, Verdi, Wagner or Robert Stolz: in July and August famous opera and operetta performances, and sometimes concerts, are projected every evening onto the gigantic screen on Rathausplatz during the Music Film Festival – if the weather plays along → **p. 109**

INSIDER TIP Incomparable Jugendstil elegance

The writer Heimito von Doderer called the 'Strudlhofstiege' with its flights of steps, ramps and Jugendstil lanterns a 'stage for the drama of life' (photo right) → **p. 51**

INSIDER TIP Imperial and bourgeois

In the Hofmobiliendepot (Imperial Furniture Collection) you can trace Habsburg domestic culture and the Viennese art of furniture-making from the 17th to 20th century → **p. 52**

INSIDER TIP Vienna's most beautiful graveyard

An ivy-covered island in the flowing river of time: the atmospheric Biedermeier Sankt Marx Cemetery with Mozart's tomb → **p. 58**

INSIDER TIP Miniature operatics

From *Aladdin* to the *Magic Flute*: after touring the palace, the Schönbrunn Marionette Theatre is well worth a visit → **p. 60**

INSIDER TIP Vienna's oldest café

Red velvet benches, cut-glass chandeliers, oriental carpets and small marble tables: guests in *Frauenhuber* feel as if they were in a plush bourgeois *salon* → **p. 65**

INSIDER TIP Shop & enjoy art

No matter whether you are looking for interior decoration, material or jewellery: *Habari* stocks high-quality, artistically crafted items from sub-Saharan Africa – and there are special exhibitions in the basement → **p. 77**

INSIDER TIP Nostalgic cinema

Paula Wessely, Hans Moser and other Austrian film stars from the Good Old Days: every day, the *Bellaria* shows tearjerkers made between or shortly after the two world wars → **p. 86**

INSIDER TIP Designer hotel

You can now spend the night in the chic but cosy five-star hotel *Das Triest* where stagecoach companies once stabled their horses → **p. 93**

INSIDER TIP Outdoor dining

A gastronomic idyll after visiting Schönbrunn: enjoy excellent suburban cooking and fine wines in the shade of chestnut trees in the inn *Zum Blauen Esel* → **p. 69**

INSIDER TIP Jungle adventure

Paddle your canoe or take a carriage ride around the Danube floodplains in the Nationalpark Donau-Auen, one of the last 'jungles' in Central Europe → **p. 60**

INSIDER TIP Lunch in the Palace

You can eat well and inexpensively in the historic surroundings of the *Soho* bistro cafeteria in the National Library complex → **p. 71**

INSIDER TIP A toast to the New Year

On the last night of the year, Vienna's inner city turns into a gigantic party playground. That is when the 'Silvesterpfad' winds its way – lined with champagne and mulled-wine booths and various stages – from the Town Hall to the Prater → **p. 109**

BEST OF ...

GREAT PLACES FOR FREE
Discover new places and save money

FOR FREE

● *How about sacred music?*
The beautiful *St Augustin Church* is famous for its solemn masses with music. You can hear festive compositions by Haydn or Schubert performed at a very high musical standard on Sundays and church holidays → p. 35

● *A morning on the Naschmarkt*
Typical Viennese atmosphere and it doesn't cost a cent. It is worth taking a walk among the lavishly decorated stands and listening to the dealers praising their wares at the top of their voices just to experience the bazaar feeling → p. 78

● *Treasures in St Stephen's Cathedral*
The interior of this magnificent Gothic building is a treasure house of priceless works of art. You can relax here after a stroll through the city and experience the unique aura of the 'most solemn sacred space on earth' (Adolf Loos) – without spending any money on a guided tour or for climbing up the tower → p. 45

● *Nature and music on the Himmelwiese*
Lie in the grass and listen to music. At weekends, classical and jazz sounds create a great atmosphere in the *Lebensbaumkreis am Himmel (Tree of Life Circle in Heaven)* – a source of natural energy on Kahlenberg. The breathtaking view of the city is also free → p. 105

● *Spectacular view from Schönbrunn Palace Park*
Of course, the palace and its state rooms are the main attraction. But a walk through the wonderful park is also a must and, by contrast, free. Don't miss the view over the western part of Vienna from the top of the hill with the 'Gloriette' → p. 59

● *Melancholic Viennese cemetery*
You can stroll between the graves of honour of geniuses such as Beethoven, Schubert and Schnitzler and feel the melancholy, morbid atmosphere that is also part of Vienna in the *Zentralfriedhof*, one of the world's largest and most beautiful cemeteries → p. 60

●●●● Dots in guidebook refer to 'Best of ...' tips

● *In the classical coffeehouse*
They are Vienna's answer to London's pubs and the bistros of Paris. The hundreds of 'public living rooms' spread throughout the city are still the epitome of everyday Viennese culture. You can feel this especially well in magnificently renovated *Central* → p. 65, 103

● *Visit the State Opera*
The 'House on the Ring' helped cement Vienna's reputation as the world's music capital. You have the opportunity of seeing and hearing opera performances of the highest standard almost every evening → p. 87

● *Fiacre ride*
Trotting through the narrow streets of the city centre or around the Ringstraße in a horse-drawn carriage is not only one of the most celebrated Viennese clichés but actually a lot of fun (photo) → p. 114

● *The Reinprecht Heuriger wine tavern*
Reinprecht in the heart of Grinzing is one of the most famous addresses where the Viennese indulge in their legendary *gemütlichkeit*. Sitting under vines, you will be able to savour the young wine and the high-calorie delicacies from the buffet → p. 64

● *Plumbing the depths of the Sigmund Freud Museum*
Even if nobody has to lie down on the couch, you can still feel a unique aura in the original rooms of the practice where the father of psychology cast light on the human soul → p. 50

● *A round on the giant Ferris wheel*
Along with 'Steffl' and Schönbrunn, this gigantic steel construction is considered a classic symbol of Vienna. Going for a ride in one of the bright red carriages is a lot of fun especially in spring when – in the words of the song – 'the flowers bloom again in the Prater' → p. 57

● *The Burgtheater – a must*
The 'Burg', as the famous theatre on the Ringstraße is known, is the flagship of theatrical art in German. No matter whether a classical play or a provocatively modern piece, a visit is always worthwhile → p. 89

ONLY IN

BEST OF ...

● *Art, coffee and cake*
You should make sure that you allow yourself enough time to visit the *Kunsthistorisches Museum* – one of the world's largest art collections – so that you can fully experience the effect made by the overpowering collection of paintings and opulent interior decoration. Afterwards, the coffee and cake served beneath the cupola will taste even better → **p. 37**

● *Exquisite sounds in the Musikverein*
As soon as you enter the 'Golden Hall' you will forget the rain and be soothed by classical music, the unbelievable acoustics and magnificent atmosphere → **p. 87**

● *Coffeehouse culture in Café Sperl*
Glass chandeliers, small marble tables, Thonet chairs and plush benches, as well as billiard tables, excellent coffee and cakes and newspapers from around the world. You will forget the time of day and the grey sky outside in this cosy typically Viennese coffeehouse → **p. 67**

● *World of music in the House of Music*
If you are expecting a traditional museum, you'll be more than surprised! An extremely entertaining, multimedia, interactive journey through the world of music awaits you in this painstakingly renovated palace where the Vienna Philharmonic Orchestra was founded in 1842 → **p. 34**

● *Dorotheum: elegant and exquisite*
The oldest pawnshop and auction house in the world is a feast for the eyes and a good place to stay dry. Have a close look at the exquisite porcelain, books, jewellery, paintings and furniture (photo) → **p. 75**

● *Hofburg – an expression of power and glory*
A tour through theImperial Palace vast former epicentre of power, will give you a first-hand impression of how much the Habsburgs loved pomp, as well as their obsession for collecting → **p. 34**

RELAX AND CHILL OUT
Take it easy and spoil yourself

● *Get back on your feet in the spa*
An ideal place to regenerate body and soul: You can refresh your weary limbs in the vast pool landscape in the *Therme Wien* and then relax and recharge your batteries in the saunas and aroma grottos → **p. 43**

● *Lie down in the MQ courtyard*
The spacious inner courtyard of the *MuseumsQuartier* has developed into a relaxation area that is popular with everybody. The gigantic lounges will tempt you to lie back and enjoy the *dolce far niente* → **p. 48**

● *Tea-time at Haas & Haas*
The traditional tea house is an ideal place to take a stylish break on your stroll through the city centre. Settle down on the comfortable rattan chairs in the shady inner courtyard and enjoy afternoon tea in Vienna → **p. 65**

● *Trip to the 'inland Adriatic'*
When you reach the *Neue Donau*, you can cycle or walk along an endless beach through completely unspoilt scenery. Find a place to relax, spread out your towel and listen to the gentle sound of the waves on the Danube → **p. 20, 58**

● *Enjoy the wine – and a bird's eye view of Vienna*
An uplifting view. Its location, surrounded by vineyards and fairy-tale views over the city are what make *Sirbu* stand out above the other *Heurige* – in the true sense of the word → **p. 65**

● *In the Herrmann Beach Bar*
It is almost as if Vienna were on the Mediterranean. In summer, the area near the mouth of the Wien River is lined with a long sandy beach complete with bar on the banks of the Danube Canal. Lulled by the sound of chic lounge music, sip the tasty drinks and enjoy the fantastic view across the Danube Canal to the new skyline of the 2nd district → **p. 39**

INTRODUCTION

DISCOVER VIENNA!

Whenever people start talking about Vienna, clichés inevitably crop up: Schönbrunn Palace, the giant Ferris wheel and St Stephen's Cathedral, *Sachertorte* with whipped cream, Lipizzaner horses, the Boys' Choir and Strauss – the 'King of the Waltz'. However, the image of a post-imperial, postcard idyll is in urgent need of an update.

Of course, it would be hard to top the splendour of the festively illuminated Ringstraße and Imperial Palace. The numerous *Heurigen* (wine taverns), *Beisln* (bars) and coffee-houses have also doggedly clung on to the remains of a royal and imperial *gemütlichkeit* from the Habsburg era. And is there any lover of music who does not go into raptures after a performance in one of the world-famous temples of the Muses such as the Musikverein or State Opera? The familiar image of sickly-sweet perfection overflowing with music – and sometimes wine – needs however to be corrected. The city on the

Photo: View of the city with the Burgtheater

Danube with its 1.67 million inhabitants has developed into Central Europe's boom-town in recent years: dynamic and self-assured, full of energy and joie de vivre – the economic motor and creative centre of a nation that, not by chance, is one of the most prosperous and successful countries in Europe and the world, and one where life is really worth living. *Heurigen* and hip hop, Sisi (Empress Elisabeth) and Schönberg, imperial pancakes and fusion cuisine – a trip to Vienna is actually two rolled into one. The

Heurigen and hip-hop, Sisi and Schönberg

first takes visitors back to the glorious past where they will be enchanted by the imperial splendour of the Ringstraße, Schönbrunn Palace and the area around St Stephen's Cathedral. The second catapults you into a multicultural metropolis in the heart of an expanding Central Europe. The miraculous rejuvenation of what was a grey, grumpy, even morbid city long after 1945 started in the mid-1970s. A large portion of the poor structural fabric from past centuries was renovated and place was even found for some showpieces of contemporary architecture – the most spectacular is probably the Haas House on Stephansplatz. In 1979, the UNO City was opened – since then, Vienna has become the third seat of the United Nations after New York and Geneva. A generously subsidised alternative cultural scene with countless small and medium-sized theatres, saw the light of day in that get-up-and-go period – along with a lively bar scene.

Donner Fountain, the most beautiful in Vienna, was built on Neuer Markt between 1737 and 1739

Vienna was given another decisive boost when the Iron Curtain fell in 1989. All of a sudden, the former imperial city found itself no longer on the outskirts of the western world but as the central cultural, political and economic hub between East and West – as it had been under the monarchy. The city, which had been governed by the Social Democrats since time immemorial until they were forced to form a coalition with the environmental party as junior partner following the communal election in 2010, received a further push towards modernity with Austria's accession to the EU in 1995. When the neighbouring countries Hungary, Slovakia and the Czech Republic acceded in 2004, Vienna once again profited from the strong links that had been forged. Finally, the renowned Mercer Studies voted Vienna the city with the world's highest quality of life in 2010. There are many reasons for this. For example, the special feeling the Viennese claim for themselves. Their *gemütlichkeit* and proverbial *schmäh*, the capability of being able to face up to an unpleasant situation with humour and make jokes about it, might also be clichés, but if you rub shoulders with one of the locals philosophising quietly after a glass or two of wine in an inn or pay attention to the regulars in one of the traditional cafés chatting over a cup of *melange* or letting the world go by as they read their newspapers, you will recognise that these notions are still valid today.

Vienna, however, is not a peaceful island in the turbulent river of time in all respects. The overall Austrian situation is naturally reflected in the federal capital as if through a magnifying glass. Some dark clouds can be made out in the (socio-)political weather forecast and some of them have been hovering over the city and country for many

A special way of looking at life: Viennese *schmäh*

years. The education situation is one of them. There has still not been a decision taken on extensive full-day schooling and a comprehensive school for all 10–14 year-olds in spite of the pupils' miserable performance in various Pisa tests. The universities also have embarrassingly poor places in international ratings. And this will possibly not change even though and Institute for Science and Technology (IST Austria), conceived as a world-class institution, was established near Klosterneuburg just beyond the city boundary in 2009. Defence is another area in which those responsible are reluctant to make long-overdue decisions, such as doing away with conscription or the country's antiquated neutrality – seen from the European-political perspective. Many find public-opinion making, which is dominated by the tabloids and a crisis-ridden national broadcasting organisation (ORF), catastrophic and the same applies to parliamentary debates. The two largest parties, the Social Democrats (SPÖ) and conservative People's Party (ÖVP), who have been transmitting images of the world and ways of life as a kind of *ersatz* religion and still govern the country in a grand coalition, are considered to be notoriously incapable and unwilling to tackle reforms and are consequently both suffering dramatic membership and electorate losses.

It might seem something of a paradox that a city and country with such handicaps could still take top rankings in many areas in international comparisons. The economic performance is splendid, exports are booming and the youth unemployment rate is far below the EU average. Social peace also appears to be guaranteed. In reality, the 'true-blue' Viennese and immigrants – most of them from Turkey, Germany, former Yugoslavia and Poland – get on much better with each other than public debate and integration policies, which were inexcusably neglected for many years, would have you believe. And, as a result, there is a very high level of public safety. It is possible to walk along Viennese streets late at night without any danger.

The quality of the air and water, woods and beaches is also impressive. The city is amazingly free of smog and dust. The luxuriant vegetation plays a major role in assuring this. Prater, Lobau, Laaer Berg, Schönbrunn, the Lainz Animal Reserve, the expansive woods between the valley of the Wien River and Leopoldsberg in the northwest and the numerous inner-city parks cover almost 50% of the 160 mi² metropolitan area. Sections of the oft-sung and oft-painted Vienna Woods that surround Vienna in the west and are up to 40km (25mi) wide in some places also act as dust filters and oxygen providers. The New Danube is especially attractive and close to the city centre; it is a unique recreational area with beaches which are as lively as Rimini on hot days and balmy summer nights, stretching for miles along its banks.

The Habsburgs reigned for 650 years

In a manner of speaking, Vienna's picturesque location is in keeping with the historical role it played in the more than 2000 years of its history. Nestling in a basin between the eastern foothills of the Alps and the western fringe of the Carpathian arch that descends to the Danube over gentle slopes, it has acted both as a bulwark against invading peoples, mainly from the east, and as a meeting place. There was an important army camp, Vindobona, here during Roman times that helped safeguard the Danube Limes, the empire's border to Germania. In the High Middle Ages, the Babenbergs had their residence here for around a century. Following that, the Habsburgs ruled their enormous realm from Vienna for almost 650 years. The city was besieged twice by the Ottoman Empire, in 1529 and 1683; both times, without success. As a consequence, Austria developed into a major power. Vienna, the eastern bastion of Christendom, whose suburbs and neighbouring villages had suffered greatly during the second siege, was reconstructed and expanded under the emperors Leopold I and Karl VI to become a magnificent Baroque metropolis with impressive churches, palaces and government buildings. Emperor Franz Joseph I freed it from its corset when he had its bastions and fortress walls demolished in 1857 and the majestic boulevard, the Ringstraße, built on the cleared space. In the second half of the 19th century, an age of massive industrialisation, the imperial city grew into a modern metropolis – one of the largest in the world at the time. The city's population reached its peak with over 2 million inhabitants in 1910.

The cultures of Central and Eastern Europe started mingling in the Danube metropolis in the 19th century. The result was that intense, creative atmosphere that found its way into intellectual history as the 'Viennese fin de siècle'. In those years, Viennese coffeehouses were crystallisation points of the European intelligentsia. Great poets including Hugo von Hofmannsthal, Franz Werfel and Josef Roth honed their linguistic skills there, Egon Erwin Kisch and Karl Kraus combated each other with their sharp pens, Bertolt Brecht and Leo Trotsky

Coffeehouses with a creative atmosphere

played chess and even Sigmund Freud dropped by regularly to have a cup of coffee and check his theories by observing live subjects. You will still get a feeling of that inspirational atmosphere in the Griensteidl, Bräunerhof, Café Central and many other traditional Viennese coffeehouses. The intellectual and artistic creativity of the

The major work of Viennese Jugendstil: the Secession building with its golden 'cabbage head' dome

city is actually still quite remarkable. The more than 9 million guests who flock to the Austrian capital every year mainly do so because of its exceptional cultural tradition – to attend a performance in the Musikverein or the State Opera where the likes of Richard Strauss, Gustav Mahler and Herbert von Karajan once conducted, to listen to the velvety sound of the Vienna Philharmonic Orchestra, or make a pilgrimage to memorial sites honouring Mozart, Beethoven, Schubert, Haydn, Léhar and all the other musicians this city inspired. But music is just one aspect of Vienna. Take a leisurely stroll along the Ringstraße, over Heldenplatz and through the narrow medieval streets; visit the Gothic and Baroque churches, the time-honoured theatres, the outstanding art museums and dazzling palaces such as Belvedere and Schönbrunn. And, go to Grinzing in the evening to taste the young wine. Or throw yourself head over heels into the turbulent nightlife in the discotheques and bars in the city centre and along the Gürtel and party the night away.

WHAT'S HOT

1 Tracking down design

Artistic events In Vienna, you can experience art with all your senses. The *Via Arte Gallery (Geibelgasse 14–16, www. viaarte.info)* goes for a mix of various forms of expression. For example, tangoing between the works. The *Galerie-rundgang (Gallery Tour) (www.galerienrundgang.at)* to the *Galerie Frey (Gluckgasse 3, www.galerie-frey.com)* and other houses revolves completely around art. Or you can explore the *Designpfad (design route)* on a double-decker bus travelling between fashionable designer shops and galleries *(www.designpfad.at, photo)*.

Tea culture 2

Asia greets Vienna If you have had your fill of coffee-houses, try a bit of Asian tea culture. *tea-licious (Margaretenstraße 22, www.tea-licious.at, photo)* specialises in tea with slimy or crispy pieces of jelly and milk or juice, so-called 'Bubble Tea'. *Cha-no-ma* highlights macha in its modern form of Japanese tea culture *(Faulmanngasse 7)*. And *Grand Cru* sells Kusmi Tea for you to take home with you *(Kaiserstraße 67, www. grandcru.at)*.

3 Vinyl lives

Record shops Do you want to pimp your record collection? Then Vienna is the right place for you! Vinyl is celebrating a comeback in well-stocked shops like *Soul Seduction (Zur Spinnerin 19, www. soulseduction.com)*. Doris Schartmüller from *Rave Up Records* can find all the rarities you are missing. The regulars know they can rely on her tips *(Hofmühlgasse 1, www.rave-up. at, photo)*. The most charming treasure trove in town? The third generation of the Teuchtler family now runs the record shop that also sells second-hand articles *(Windmühlgasse 10)*.

A bit of country in the city

Green Vienna It's not a joke! You can experience the country in the middle of town. Workshops and guided tours in the *Biosphärenpark Wiener Wald (Vienna Woods Biosphere Park)* take you out into the open on 'herb hikes' and other excursions *(www.bpww.at, photo)*. Plant lovers will find what they like most on the tours and workshops held in the *Palmenhaus* and *Blumengärten Hirschstetten* from the mid-April–mid-October – advance booking necessary *(www.wien.gv.at)*. Looking for recreation close to town? How about the new Lumbyepark or Asperner Heustadelpark as many people call it *(next to Sophie-Scholl-Gasse 8)*? Nature-lovers make winter seem not quite so long at the *Blumenball* in the Town Hall. The event started out as a get-together for the city council's gardeners but has now developed into one of the most popular balls in town *(www.ballkalender.cc)*.

4

Fashion Vienna Style

5

The mixture makes the difference Vienna's young designers take risks and their boutiques are off-beat. Lena Hoschek *(Gutenberggasse 17, www. lenahoschek.com)* and Susanne Bisovsky *(e.g. at Sisi Vienna, Annagasse 11, www.bisovsky.com)* combine elements of traditional costumes with punk accessories to create dashing clothes. Fashion victims will feel right at home in *Mon Ami*. Young fashion makers present and sell their creations in the back rooms of the Café Atelier. You can even see some of them at work *(Theobaldgasse 9, www. monami.at)*. The latest collections by newcomers and the city's established designers are sold in the unique environment of the *Samstag Shop (Margaretenstraße 46, www.samstag-shop.com, photo)*.

IN A NUTSHELL

ARCHITECTURE

There are two sides to Vienna's cityscape. On the one hand there is the time-honoured centre with charmingly old-fashioned silhouettes of Gothic and Historicist towers, Baroque domes and a sea of tile-roofed houses from the Biedermeier era and the period of rapid industrial expansion in the latter part of the 19th century known as the *Gründerzeit*. This is where the vast and imposing Hofburg (Imperial Palace) is located from where the Habsburgs ruled half of Europe for a period. There are even some scattered remnants of buildings from the Roman camp of Vindobona.

On the other hand, for some years now, the skyline of a second, ultramodern urban environment has been sprouting up on the other side of the Danube. The Andromeda and Millennium Towers, the UNO City (with Heinz Tesar's new church at its feet) and Austria Center, the Donau City residential park, the Tech Gate technology centre, as well as a host of other office and apartment towers show just how dynamic the former imperial city has remained and delight fans of modern architecture. Hans Hollein, Gustav Peichl, Harry Seidler and Coop Himmelb(l)au are just some of the most prominent architects who have created these buildings.

Between hip-hop and the Habsburgs, Biedermeier and Kruder & Dorfmeister: Vienna from classic to really way-out

CABARET

As with so many other genres in the lively artistic scene, the roots of today's cabaret lie in the 1980s. Helmut Qualtinger, the progenitor of the Viennese post-war satirical cabaret and creator of the immortal figure of the prototypical everyday fascist 'Herr Karl', was still alive when this form of socio-critical cabaret experienced its first boom. The young audience enjoyed eating, drinking, smoking and laughing out loud during performances – and feeling that they were being critical citizens at the same time.

Since then, the local cabaret scene has developed into a mass movement – without lowering the quality. More than a dozen theatres, from the small *Niedermair Theatre* to the gigantic tent of the *Palais Novak* or the *Stadtsaal* that was opened

Coffee with the imperial couple: Franz Joseph and Sisi on the walls of the Café Central

in 2011, specialise in satirical cabaret. On some evenings, as many as 2500 tickets are sold.

Sometimes the borderline to theatre becomes blurred. Stars such as Josef Hader and Thomas Maurer, for example, have a made a name for themselves as actor-cum-writers of solo performances in which they play a role and not themselves. However, others like Karl Ferdinand Kratzl, Alf Poier and Martin Puntigam or the successful duo of stand-up comedians Stermann & Grissemann, rely on considerably more vitriolic comedy and oddball staging.

If you speak German well enough, there is no need to worry that you will not understand the Viennese dialect. Most of the satirists today speak German in a way that can be understood beyond the city limits.

DANUBE

In spite of the name of the famous waltz, Vienna did not lie on the 'beautiful blue Danube' but next to it for centuries. It was not until the end of the 19th century when the river – it is really a greyish brown, by the way – was regulated so that the city and Danube actually came close to each other. The relationship became really intimate in the 1970s when a second riverbed was excavated in order to prevent flooding once and for all. And, with it, an island was created – 600ft wide and 20km (13mi) long – that was immediately developed into a recreational area, a gigantic inland Adriatic, that has since become extremely popular with the Viennese. Cyclists, hikers, joggers and inline skaters love the long, asphalted paths on the ● Donauinsel (Danube

Island). Scouts and barbecue fans prepare their food at special locations on the banks. Next to them, anglers dream of making the catch of their life.

At the height of summer, this artificial 'natural' landscape turns into something of a Central European version of Rimini. That is when sun worshippers take over the lawns and sand-and-gravel beaches, go for a pedal-boat trip, water ski and play street soccer, basketball and beach volleyball. And after the sun sets a – mainly young – crowd has fun all night long in the numerous restaurants, bars and discos on the entertainment strip *Copa Cagrana* named after the nearby Kagran district.

HABSBURGS

They disappeared from the scene more than 90 years ago. But the legend of this dynasty that ruled an empire from Vienna for more than 600 years is still (almost) as alive as if the emperor himself were still in power. A quick glance at the shelves in any bookshop proves this – there are stacks and stacks of biographies on Maria Theresa, Crown Prince Rudolf and Sisi. And it is no mere coincidence that there are always fresh flowers in front of some of the sarcophaguses in the Imperial Crypt. It is no mere coincidence that a museum devoted entirely to Empress Elisabeth was opened. Not without reason that some of the company signs on the exclusive shopping streets still show the 'k. u. k. Hoflieferant' (Purveyor to the Imperial and Royal Court) emblem, that souvenir shops sell confectionery and t-shirts in the black-and-yellow heraldic colours of the Habsburgs, and that today the fiacre drivers still grow long bushy sideburns so that they will look as much like Emperor Franz Joseph as possible. What is behind all this? Commercial considerations of course and, for a small majority, maybe even genuine political nostalgia. But, for must Viennese it is probably only the attitude they are accustomed to showing to everything from the past: posthumous glorification. The Viennese satirist Helmut Qualtinger described it perfectly: 'In Vienna, you have to die before you can become famous. Once you're dead, you can almost live forever.'

MULTICULTURE

The contradictoriness in the soul of the Viennese becomes apparent in their relationship to 'foreigners' who now make up around 18% of the population. On the one hand, the xenophobic statements of Heinz-Christian Strache, the successor to the professional agitator Jörg Haider who was killed in a car crash in 2008, and others of that ilk, still find alarmingly fertile ground – especially in the capital. A through-and-through Viennese finds it easy to forget that there is usually at least one Hungarian uncle or Bohemian grandmother somewhere in the family tree.

On the other hand, a look at Vienna's streets, squares and markets will suffice for you to recognise immediately the pragmatic tolerance of the way in which this city integrates its immigrants. Greek and Turkish merchants sell olives and pita bread next to each other without any problems. Many Arabs and Iranians who came to Vienna to study medicine remained and are now highly-respected practicing doctors. And many of the families of the foreign workers who came to Austria from Croatia, Serbia and Turkey are now 'documented and certified' Viennese whose children are completely in command of the soft, drawn out vowels of the local dialect.

It is therefore no surprise that, relative to the size of the country's population, the

Viennese are so proud that Austria took in more refugees from Hungary in 1956, from Czechoslovakia in 1968 and from former-Yugoslavia in the 1990s than any other country in Europe. And also that, until today, racist mobbing, which has led to violence elsewhere, has remained almost completely unknown in Vienna.

MUSIC

Strauss waltzes and the State Opera are probably old hat for young visitors to the city. But Vienna also does not have to give up its position as the world's capital of music when it comes to the house and hip-hop generation. That is because, out of earshot of the highly praised tones of classical music, a top-class contemporary scene has established itself – you could almost say furtively. Its roots go back to the pop minstrels of the 1970s including Wolfgang Ambros and Rainhard Fendrich who are still active today. In the 1980s, Falco reached the number one position in the American charts and showed that there was something like genuine rap 'made in Austria'. And at the beginning of the new millennium, local sampling and remixing gods like Kruder & Dorfmeister, Pulsinger & Tunakan and THE WAZ Experience sky-rocketed into the international electronic heavens. Since then, it has been almost impossible to finish off a bout of Viennese nightlife without being bowled over by the crazy sound creations of star DJs of this kind – or even some up-and-coming desperado at the mixing console.

WATER

You will notice just how high the quality of life in Vienna is as soon as you turn on the tap. In contrast to many other large cities where chlorinated water from underground or even wastewater treatment plants pours out, in Vienna you have crystal-clear, delicious drinking water from high up in the mountains. The Viennese have the geologist Eduard Suess to thank for this. More than 130 years ago – and against massive resistance from the authorities – he developed the visionary project of laying water pipes from mountain springs and since then water has flown uninterruptedly through many tunnels and over aqueducts for the 90km (56mi) from the Kaiserbrunnen (Emperor's Spring) in the Rax and Schneeberg region to the Austrian capital. Since 1910, a second similarly-long pipeline has brought additional mountain water from the Hochschwab area in Styria to Vienna. Together, these pioneering installations have had a negative influence on the turnover of the local producers of mineral water.

WINE

One of Vienna's less well-known attractions is its wine. Of course, the *Heurigen* (wine taverns), with their hearty food and schmaltzy songs to go along with the wine, are legendary and well-patronised. But it is only slowly being registered that excellent wines are not only drunk in the outer districts but also grown and pressed there. Some of them have already been awarded renowned prizes. There is probably no other capital city in the world that has such a history of wine-growing culture reaching so far back into the past. And definitely none where so many innovative winegrowers are at work.

The Celts used the fertile soil and warm, dry climate at the eastern edge of the Alps for winegrowing as long as 2500 years ago. In the Roman period, Emperor Probus introduced new varieties and methods of cultivation. And, in the Middle Ages, the Viennese almost drowned in wine. According to old chronicles, as much as 120 litres per head were swilled down every year.

Vines in Klosterneuburg near Vienna, one of the oldest wine-growing estates in Austria

Wine was even used in the mortar for St Stephen's Cathedral.

Phylloxera, together with high taxes and the competition from coffee and beer which had become the fashionable drinks of the period, almost put an end to local winegrowing. Until recently, quantity was considered more important than quality. Hectolitres of Grüner Veltliner, far and away the most popular variety, were mixed with soda water and, served in the typical quarter-litre glasses with a handle, found their way down thirsty throats as the so-called *G'spritzter*. Oenological connoisseurs would probably look with disdain at this rustic way of drinking wine.

Today, 230 *Weinhauer* – the Austrian term for winegrowers – cultivate an area of almost 2000 acres planted with vines. The harvest results in up to 2 million litres (70,000ft³) of wine – 80% of it white – and more than two thirds are sold locally. Recently, an increasing number of growers have been paying greater attention to improving the quality. Fritz Wieninger, Rainer Christ, Michael Edlmoser and Richard Zahel are among the most outstanding of these pioneers. They run chic *Heurigen* along with their innovative vineyards. And together with other comrades in arms, they cooperate with the City of Vienna in a series of events – from grape blossom festivals and picnics in the vineyards, wine tasting and seminars, to evenings of Viennese song and wine hikes. The annual highlight is the impressively staged awarding of the Viennese Wine Prize and tasting of the top wines held in the courtyard of the Town Hall at the end of June or early in July *(www.wienerweinpreis.at)*. Additional information: *www.wienerwein.at*.

THE PERFECT DAY
Vienna in 24 hours

07:45am ONCE AROUND THE RING

It's worth getting up early! The best time to get onto a Line 1 tram is before the rush hour begins. It is difficult to think of a better way to become acquainted with the splendour of the Habsburg metropolis. Travelling along the *Ringstraße* → p. 43 you will pass the State Opera, Parliament and Town Hall shining in the early morning light until you finally reach the Donaukanal and make the return trip.

08:30am COFFEEHOUSE & NASCHMARKT

This is followed by a short break to have a bite to eat in a classic coffeehouse, the *Sperl* → p. 67. Order a *melange* and a *rescher* (crispy) emperor's roll and 'an egg in a glass'. Fortified, go down to the 'belly of Vienna', the *Naschmarkt* → p. 78 (photo left) where there are mountains of fruit, vegetables and all kinds of delicacies. They are not only there to be looked at; you should try some of the little snacks.

09:30am SCHÖNBRUNN

Take the U4 underground from Kettenbrückengasse at the end of the Naschmarkt and you will reach *Schönbrunn* → p. 59 in just a few minutes. A tour through the state rooms in the palace is an absolute must. But you should also take a walk through the extensive park and go up to the Gloriette. If there is enough time left, a visit to the *Zoo* → p. 60 is a good option – the oldest one in the world.

12:00pm LUNCH WITH A VIEW

Is your stomach rumbling? Back to town (tram 58 and then U3) where you will find several restaurants in the *MuseumsQuartier* → p. 48. In spite of its excellent cooking, the chic *Halle Café-Restaurant* → p. 65 is inexpensive and is a good choice for lunch with a view down on the MQ courtyard.

01:00pm EXQUISITE ART EXPERIENCE

After a satisfying meal, it is time to tackle one of the first-class museums of your list. Lovers of Schiele, Klimt & Co. head for the *Leopold Museum* → p. 49; those who are more interested in contemporary art to the *Museum Moderner Kunst* → p. 49; and it is only a two-minute walk across the road to the *Kunsthistorisches Museum* → p. 37 if you prefer Old Masters of the very highest quality.

Get to know some of the most dazzling, exciting and relaxing facets of Vienna – all in a single day

`03:00pm` SHOPPING

The time has come for a shopping spree. Cross Maria-Theresienplatz and Heldenplatz and wander along Stallburggasse and its side streets until you reach *Kärntner Straße → p. 72*. But be careful: your holiday budget will be in great danger as you look in the windows of the antique, fashion and arts-and-crafts shops.

`04:00pm` ST STEPHEN'S CATHEDRAL

Are you prepared for Vienna's number one attraction? Both the inside and out of *St Stephen's Cathedral → p. 45* are a Gothic miracle and call for a thorough inspection. Go down into the catacombs or – more uplifting – to the Tower Keeper's Room with a spectacular view over Vienna.

`05:00pm` OLD CITY STROLL

As you stroll westwards over the Graben, Hof and Freyung to Schottenring, you will pass churches steeped in history including the Baroque *St Peter's Church → p. 43*. Halfway along the route, you should make a break in the shopping arcade in *Palais Ferstel → p. 42* where you can also have dinner in the famous *Café Central → p. 65*.

`07:30pm` OPERA OR DRAMA?

A performance in the famous *State Opera → p. 87* (photo above) is next on the music fan's programme; if you are more interested in the theatre and your German is good enough, you should try to get tickets for the renowned *Burgtheater → p. 89* or the smaller alternative, the *Akademietheater → p. 89*.

`10:00pm` CHILL OUT

Night owls are now probably looking for an exciting way to end the long day. Aesthetes can sip excellent drinks and admire the authentic Jugendstil atmosphere until the early hours of the morning in the *Loos Bar → p. 83*. If you want to dance in chic surroundings with top DJs, go under the Ringstraße to *Passage → p. 84*.

Underground to the starting point: U1, U2, U4. Stop: Oper (State Opera) Save money with a day ticket for public transportation (6.70 euros)

SIGHTSEEING

WHERE TO START?

The **square in front of the Staatsoper (126 C5)** (*K9*): The most important museums are just a few minutes' walk away. Trams leave from here for the **Ringstraße**; in five minutes, you can be in front of **St Stephen's** or on the **Naschmarkt**. The U1, U2 and U4 underground lines, as well as trams 1, 2, D and 62, all stop in the Karlsplatz/Opera area. One place to park is in the 'Park & Ride' multi-storey in Hütteldorf at the terminus of the U4.

Vienna makes it easy for visitors to get their bearings. The heart of the city is formed by the medieval centre: the First District, or Inner City. And, in the middle, Vienna's number one symbol St Stephen's Cathedral towers into the sky.

Several other Romanesque and Gothic churches bear witness to the deep Catholic roots of the imperial city. Many of the major monuments are on the Ringstraße, Vienna's showpiece boulevard, which was built on the site of the city walls that were demolished in the middle of the 19th century. Any sightseeing tour should begin in the 500-acre historical city centre; the best way to get around is on foot as

Photo: Schönbrunn Palace

Schönbrunn and St Stephen's Cathedral, the Ringstraße and Belvedere: famous jewels in the former imperial city

many sections are closed to traffic. A ride in a fiacre is atmospheric but not exactly inexpensive. You can also see the splendid buildings on the Ringstraße in comfort out of the windows of trams 1 and 2.

The sights become scarcer as you move further afield. The Prater recreation area on the other side of the Danube Canal is in the Second District. The Third is considered the 'Embassy Quarter' and the Eighth

a sanctuary for the upper middle-classes not far from the centre. These former villages on the outskirts of Vienna are surrounded by the Gürtel, a six-lane major thoroughfare that is currently being improved.

Vienna has many more than 100 museums – from world-famous collections such as those in the 'Kunsthistorisches', the Treasury in the Hofburg and the collections

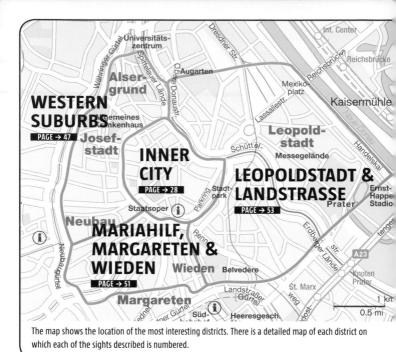

The map shows the location of the most interesting districts. There is a detailed map of each district on which each of the sights described is numbered.

of Austrian architecture, to small institutions which are well worth visiting, such as those commemorating Johann Strauss, Franz Schubert and Joseph Haydn. The city has the power of the old Habsburgs to thank for this wealth. The emperors were the ones who, with their appetite for collecting, brought together paintings and other objets d'art from all over the empire, employed skilled craftsmen and sent explorers to the four corners of the globe to bring back natural treasures and works of art. A second reason for the great variety in the museum landscape lies in the Viennese love of curiosities. There is the Museum of Art Fakes and the Undertakers' Museum, an orthopaedic museum for animals with hooves and claws, and one for pathological, anatomical specimens.

To make orientation easier, more than 200 artistically and historically interesting buildings are marked with signs, decorated with a red-and-white flag, giving the most important information on the particular building.

INNER CITY

The historical core of Vienna, which the locals simply call 'the First', is not only the geographical and administrative centre of the city. It is also the star of all the 23 districts when it comes to tourist attractions.

Most of the main sights can be found along the Ringstraße, in the side streets from the late 19th century that branch off of it, as if they had been drawn using a ruler, and in the medieval labyrinth around St Stephen's Cathedral. Two or three decades ago the city centre was threatened with being deserted after closing hours as everybody raced off home. There is no trace of that anymore. The pedestrian precinct with its elegant shops, the booming pub scene, the renovated historical buildings, as well as countless artistic initiatives make sure that there is never a dull moment.

■ 1 INSIDER TIP ► AKADEMIE DER BILDENDEN KÜNSTE
(126 C5) (⌗ K9)

The Academy of Fine Arts, in the style of the High Renaissance, is decorated with terracotta and frescoes and is home to the world-famous picture gallery with a representative selection of western art from six centuries. Hans Baldung Grien, Lucas Cranach the Elder, Titian, Sandro Botticelli, Giovanni Battista Tiepolo, Peter Paul Rubens, Rembrandt and Anthony van Dyck are just some of the masters whose works are on display here. The absolute highlight of the collection is the triptych *The Last Judgement* by Hieronymus Bosch, a magnificent fireworks display of fascinating, but cruel, phantasmagorical scenes. The associated Kupferstichkabinett (Cabinet of Prints and Drawings) has several hundred pictures from the Biedermeier period, as well as medieval architectural drawings. *Tue–Sun & holidays 10am–6pm | entrance fee 8 euros | Schillerplatz 3 | www.akademiegalerie.at | tram1, 2 Burgring, bus 57A, U1, U2, U4 Karlsplatz*

■ 2 ALBERTINA (126 C4) (⌗ K9)

The Palais Albertina, named after its builder, Duke Albert von Sachsen-Teschen, one of Empress Maria Theresa's sons-in-law, on Augustinerstraße diagonally behind the State Opera, has the world's largest collection of graphic art. It contains 60,000 drawings and watercolours as well as around 1.5 million prints from

---

★ Hofburg
The heart of the empire → p. 34

★ Kunsthistorisches Museum
Magnificent building on the Ringstraße with countless masterpieces by Titian, Bruegel, Rembrandt, etc. → p. 37

★ Ringstraße
Parade of late-19th-century monumental architecture on Vienna's showcase boulevard → p. 43

★ Schatzkammer
Priceless Habsburg heirlooms and other valuable exhibits → p. 44

★ Stephansdom
Vienna's Gothic cathedral → p. 45

★ MuseumsQuartier
Vienna's most recent top attraction with more than 20 museums → p. 48

★ Belvedere
Prince Eugene's fairy-tale palace → p. 54

★ Prater
Green oasis for fun and sport, with an amusement park and giant Ferris wheel → p. 57

★ Grinzing
Heurigen gemütlichkeit under chestnut trees in the famous wine-growing village in the Vienna Woods → p. 57

★ Schönbrunn Palace
The Habsburgs' charming summer residence → p. 59

MARCO POLO HIGHLIGHTS

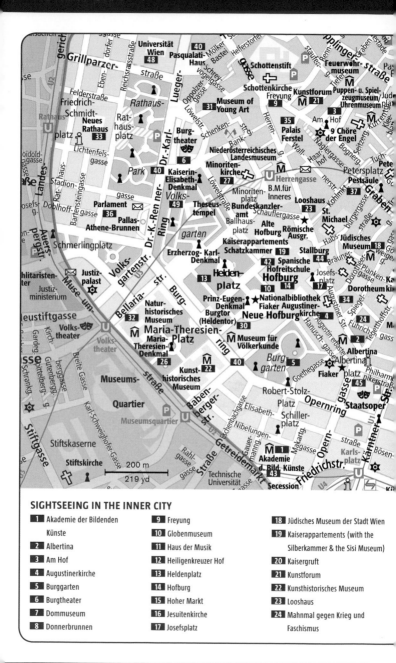

SIGHTSEEING IN THE INNER CITY

1 Akademie der Bildenden Künste

2 Albertina

3 Am Hof

4 Augustinerkirche

5 Burggarten

6 Burgtheater

7 Dommuseum

8 Donnerbrunnen

9 Freyung

10 Globenmuseum

11 Haus der Musik

12 Heiligenkreuzer Hof

13 Heldenplatz

14 Hofburg

15 Hoher Markt

16 Jesuitenkirche

17 Josefsplatz

18 Jüdisches Museum der Stadt Wien

19 Kaiserappartements (with the Silberkammer & the Sisi Museum)

20 Kaisergruft

21 Kunstforum

22 Kunsthistorisches Museum

23 Looshaus

24 Mahnmal gegen Krieg und Faschismus

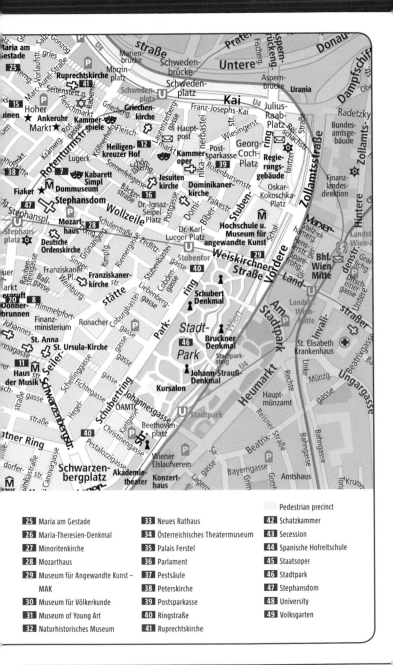

almost all of the artists active in the past 600 years. Their sensitivity to light makes it impossible to show them permanently. 500 works of classical modern art from the Batliner Collection are on display in the painstakingly renovated building and temporary exhibitions with works by the greatest masters – from Rembrandt to Schiele – are held regularly. *Daily 10am– 6pm, Wed to 9pm | entrance fee 9.50 euros | Augustinerstraße | www.albertina. at | tram D, 1, 2, 62, 65, bus 59A, U1, U2, U4 Karlsplatz/Oper*

🔳 AM HOF (126 C2–3) (*ⓂK8*)

The 'Hof' – the court of the Dukes of Babenberg – already stood in the former centre of the city in the 12th century. A good 100 years later, the ruler's seat moved to the Hofburg but the square's feudal flair has been preserved to this day. The Mariensäule (Column of the Virgin Mary) in the centre of the square is surrounded by a series of impressive façades: the 'Church of the Nine Choirs of Angels' with Palais Collalto, where Mozart gave his first concert in Vienna, to the left; opposite *(No. 8)*, the Marklein House, designed by J.L. von Hildebrandt and the 'Citizens' Armoury' with the *Fire Brigade Museum at No. 10 | Sun & holidays 9am– noon, weekdays, by appointment | tel. 53 19 90). Am Hof | bus 1 A*

🔳 AUGUSTINERKIRCHE (126 C4) (*ⓂK8–9*)

St Augustin's, dating from the 1330s, is a Gothic hall church with beautiful rib and net vaulted ceilings. It served the Habsburgs as the parish church for their court from the middle of the 17th century. This is where the imperial family's offspring were christened and it is also where many of them – including Emperor Franz Joseph and Sisi – stepped up to the altar. The main highlights of the three-naved interior are the marble tomb of Archduchess Maria Christine, created by the Classicist sculptor Antonio Canova, and the Gothic St George's Chapel. *Augustinerstraße 3 | Tram D, 1, 2, U1, U2, U4 Karlsplatz*

🔳 BURGGARTEN (126 C4–5) (*ⓂK9*)

Laid out for the exclusive use of the imperial family in 1818, the Court Garden opened its gates to the public 100 years later. You can stroll past monuments to Mozart and the two emperors Franz I Stephan of Lorraine and Franz Joseph I in the extremely well cared-for complex. The Palmenhaus, with a chic café-brasserie and lovely terrace, is also worth visiting. *March–Dec Mon–Sat 10am–1am, Sun & holidays 10am–midnight | Burgring/ Opernring | tram D, 1, 2, bus 57A*

🔳 BURGTHEATER (126 B3) (*ⓂJ8*)

Not only what happens on stage makes this temple of German thespian culture interesting. The building itself is well worth a visit. It was built in 1874–88 to plans by Gottfried Semper and Carl von Hasenauer, with a façade in the style of the Italian High Renaissance, colossal busts of great poets over the windows and a spectacular interior with ceremonial staircases, refreshment rooms and seating for 1500. *Dr.-Karl-Lueger-Ring 2 | guided tours (approx. 1 hour) daily 3pm | entrance fee 5.50 euros | tram D, 1, 2 Rathausplatz*

🔳 DOMMUSEUM (127 D3) (*ⓂL8*)

The Cathedral Museum displays the medieval treasures in the cathedral's possession: Gothic panel paintings and statues, reliquaries, glass windows and liturgical vessels. The portrait of Duke Rudolf IV, the founder of the University and St Stephen's Cathedral, painted around 1365, is considered the first individual portrait north of the Alps. *Wed–Sat 10am–6pm, Tue*

Exclusive shopping arcade in the Venetian-style Palais Ferstel on the Freyung

10am–8pm | entrance fee 7 euros | Stephansplatz 6 | passage | www.dom museum.at | U1, U3 Stephansplatz

▣ DONNERBRUNNEN
(127 D4) (*ℳ K8*)

Vienna's most beautiful fountain, the Donner Fountain, was created in 1737–39 – a masterpiece by the great Baroque sculptor Georg Raphael Donner. The statue in the centre shows Prudence, the allegory of caution. The figures around the edge of the pool personify the four main tributaries of the Danube in Austria – the Traun, Enns, Ybbs and March Rivers. Donner's lead sculptures were replaced by bronze copies in the 19th century; the originals are in the Baroque Museum in the Lower Belvedere. *Neuer Markt | bus 3A, U1, U3 Stephansplatz*

▣ FREYUNG
(126 C2) (*ℳ K8*)

In the Middle Ages, the large, triangular open space in the northwest of the Old Town served as a marketplace, a stage for clowns and an execution site. The Babenberg Duke Heinrich II Jasomirgott founded the Schottenstift benedictine abbey on the north side in 1155. Many magnificent palaces for the nobility were built around the Freyung – including the Baroque Palais Daun-Kinsky (*No. 4*) designed by Lukas von Hildebrandt, as well as Palais Harrach (*No. 3*) and the Venetian-style Palais Ferstel (*No. 2*) with the famous *Café Central*. You should also take a closer look at the so-called Schubladenhaus (Chest-of-Drawers House) to the right of the Schottenkirche. *Bus 1A, U3, Herrengasse*

10 GLOBENMUSEUM (126 C3) *(ɯ K8)*

The only museum of its kind in the world – with more than 450 globes and globe-like instruments in the lovingly restored Palais Mollard. This is also the site of the Esperanto and Papyrus Museums. *Tue–Wed and Fri–Sat 10am–6pm, Thu 10am–9pm | entrance fee 5 euros | combined ticket with state hall in the Nationalbibliothek, Esperanto*

12 HEILIGENKREUZER HOF
(127 E3) *(ɯ L8)*

Similar to many other monasteries in Lower Austria, the Cistercian Heiligenkreuz also has property in Vienna. Sections of this court-like complex are more than 800 years old. The monastery courtyard was built in the 17th century and gained its present appearance in the 18th century.

The Hofburg: the Habsburgs' labyrinthine home with 2500 rooms and 19 courtyards

and Papyrus Museums 12 euros | Herrengasse 9 | www.onb.ac.at | bus 2A, 3A, U3 Herrengasse

Its inner courtyard is very tranquil and atmospheric. *Schönlaterngasse 5/Grashofgasse 3 | bus 2 A*

11 HAUS DER MUSIK ●
(127 D5) *(ɯ L9)*

Visitors take an interactive journey through the world of sound – from the Vienna Philharmonic Orchestra that was founded here in 1842 to hyper-instruments to experiment with – on the seven floors of this carefully renovated palais. *Daily 10am–10pm | entrance fee 11 euros | Seilerstätte 30 | www.hdm.at | tram D, 1, 2, 71 Schubertring, U1, U2, U4 Karlsplatz*

13 HELDENPLATZ ☼
(126 B–C4) *(ɯ J–K 8–9)*

The unique panoramic view sweeps from the semi-circle of the Neue Burg over Heldenplatz with the long Baroque façade of the Leopoldine Wing and the two extravagant equestrian statues of Archduke Karl and Prince Eugene of Savoy and further to the Volksgarten with the silhouette of the Rathaus and Burgtheater to the Kahlenberg hill in the distance. The Äussere

Burgtor (outer castle gate), which separates this gigantic, mostly lawned area from the Ringstraße, was created by Peter von Nobile (1824) to commemorate the Battle of Leipzig. *Heldenplatz | tram D, 1, 2, bus 2A, U3 Herrengasse*

14 HOFBURG ★ ●
(126 B–C 3–4) (⌘ K 8–9)
For more than 600 years – from when the Habsburg king Rudolf I received feudal rights to the lands of Austria (1276) until the abdication of Emperor Karl (1918) – the Imperial Palace (the 'Burg') was the residence of the Austrian dynasty. Initially a comparatively small castle, it increased in size over the centuries in keeping with the power and extent of its residents' empire, to become the labyrinthine complex of buildings with 18 wings and 19 courtyards that exists today.

The Schweizerhof is the oldest section from where one enters the Schatzkammer (Treasury) and Burgkapelle (Court Chapel). The Stallburg, Amalientrakt and red-black-and-gold Schweizertor at the entrance to the court of the same name were created in the 16th century. The Leopoldinische Trakt was added in the 17th century, followed in the 18th by the Reichskanzleitrakt (Imperial Chancellor's Wing), built under the direction of Johann Lukas von Hildebrandt and Joseph Emanuel Fischer von Erlach. Father and son Fischer von Erlach also created the Winterreitschule where the Lipizzaner horses of the Spanish Riding School perform, as well as the Nationalbibliothek. Many consider its Baroque Prunksaal (State Hall) with its enormous dome the world's most beautiful library. The Michaelertrakt was completed at the end of the 19th century. And finally, the Neue Burg was built between 1891 and 1913 as part of a major expansion project that was not completed on account of World War I.

Only a tiny portion of the approximately 2500 rooms in this labyrinth of stone can be visited. These include the Kaiserappartements (Imperial Apartments) with the Sisi Museum as well as the Silberkammer (Silver Collection). Both are accessible from the entrance beneath the dome in the Michaelertrakt. Then the Schatzkammer, the Burgkapelle, the Prunksaal in the Nationalbibliothek, the Spanish Riding School and finally the Hofjagd und Rüstkammer (Collection of Arms and Armour), the collection of ancient musical instruments, the Museum of Ethnology and the Ephesus Museum – all belonging to the Kunsthistorisches Museum – in the Neue Burg. Today, the Hofburg also houses the Chancellery of the Federal President, a very busy congress centre, various offices, private and official apartments as well as some shops in the pedestrian passage

LOW BUDGET

▶ On the first Sun in the month, no admission is charged to the permanent exhibitions in the 18 city museums (including the main *Wien Museum Karlsplatz* and *musicians' memorial rooms)*. Children up to the age of 19 never have to pay an entrance fee to any state museums (including *Albertina, Kunsthistorisches Museum* and *Naturhistorisches Museum)*.

▶ First rate performances of ● sacred music and that free of charge: every Sun at 11am in the beautiful Gothic Augustinerkirche **(126 C4)** *(⌘ K 8–9)*. *Augustinerstraße 3 | www.augustiner kirche.at | tram D, 1, 2, U1, U2, U4 Karlsplatz*

between the Burghof and Heldenplatz. *Michaelerplatz, Josefsplatz, Heldenplatz, Ballhausplatz. Nationalbibliothek: Josefsplatz 1 | Tue–Sun 10am–6pm, Thu 10am–9pm | entrance fee 7 euros | www.hofburgwien.at | www.onb.ac.at | tram D, 1, 2 Burgring, bus 2A, 3A, U1, U2, U4 Karlsplatz, U3*

15 HOHER MARKT (127 D2–3) *(ᗷ L8)*
Foundations and sections of the wall of the Roman legions' camp Vindobona *(Römermuseum | Tue–Sun 9am–6pm)* were discovered underneath the pavement of the oldest square in Vienna which was also the site of the dungeons, pillory and city court building in the Middle Ages. The remains of officers' houses can be seen in the subterranean showroom. In 1911, the Jugendstil artist Franz von Matsch joined the buildings at Nos. 10 and 11 with a bridge-like construction and an artistic clock. 12 figures from the history of Vienna appear over 12 hours and there is a parade of the entire group, complete with music, every day at noon. *Bus 2A, 3A, U1, U3 Stephansplatz*

16 INSIDER TIP JESUITENKIRCHE (127 E3) *(ᗷ L8)*
The most fascinating aspect of the Jesuite Church is its illusionist ceiling painting that creates the impression of a dome in the middle of the nave. The church (also known as the University Church) was built in the 17th century before being redecorated in the High Baroque style by Andrea Pozzo in the early 18th century. Its two-towered façade lines one of the most charming squares in the city centre. *Dr.-Ignaz-Seipel-Platz | tram 1, 2, bus 2A, U3 Stubentor*

17 INSIDER TIP JOSEFSPLATZ (126 C4) *(ᗷ K8)*
This impressive, architecturally homogenous square in the city centre is domi-

nated by the long façade of the Nationalbibliothek. The square is framed on the opposite side by the Classicist Palais Pallavicini *(No. 5)* and Palais Palffy with its Renaissance façade *(No. 6)*. *Bus 2A*

18 JÜDISCHES MUSEUM DER STADT WIEN (126 C4) *(ᗷ K8)*
A permanent exhibition of Jewish religious history and suffering, as well as temporary shows dealing with Jewish literature, architecture, photography, etc. *Sun–Fri and holidays 10am–6pm | entrance fee 6.50 euros | Dorotheergasse 11 | www.jmw.at | U1, U3 Stephansplatz*

19 KAISERAPPARTEMENTS (WITH SILBERKAMMER & SISI MUSEUM) (126 C3–4) *(ᗷ K8)*
This is how dinner was served at the Viennese court: on fine china from eastern Asia, Sèvres and Augarten, with cut glass and silver cutlery. The highlight is the almost 100ft-long Milanese table centrepiece and a state dining service for 140 people. The Imperial Apartments include the private rooms of Emperor Franz Joseph I and his wife Elisabeth, their dining room, audience hall, the quarters of the imperial officers' corps, the conference room as well as the apartments where Tsar Alexander I resided during the Congress of Vienna. The *Sisi Museum* is also part of this complex and shows the 'truth and not the myth' about Empress Elisabeth, alias Sisi, who has been transfigured into something of a legend. *Sept–June daily 9am–5.30pm, July/Aug daily 9am–6pm | entrance fee 10.50 euros (incl. Sisi Museum) | Sisi Ticket in combination with Schönbrunn, Hofburg and Imperial Furniture Collection 23.50 euros | Innerer Burghof, Kaisertor | www.hofburg-wien.at | bus 2A, U1, U3 Stephansplatz; U3 Herrengasse*

20 KAISERGRUFT
(127 D4) *(🚇 K8–9)*

Since 1632, all Habsburg rulers and their closest relatives have been buried here in the Imperial Crypt underneath the Capuchin Church. But their hearts have found their final resting place in St Augustin's Church and their internal organs in the catacombs of St Stephen's. The last emperor to be buried here was

21 KUNSTFORUM (126 C2) *(🚇 K8)*

Temporary exhibitions of top quality 19th and 20th-century art are shown in the rooms designed by star architect Gustav Peichl. *Sat–Thu 10am–7pm, Fri 10am–9pm | entrance fee 9 euros, 'happy hour' Mon–Thu (except holidays) 6–7pm: two people for the price of one | Freyung 8 | www.kunstforum-wien.at | tram D, 1, U2 Schottentor, U3 Herrengasse*

Imperial Crypt: the opulently decorated sarcophaguses of Maria Theresa and Franz Stephan

Franz Joseph I after his death in 1916. The last burial of a crowned head, however, took place in 1989 when Empress Zita, Karl I's widow, was laid to rest here. The most magnificent of the 138 coffins is the double sarcophagus Balthasar Ferdinand Moll created for Maria Theresa and her husband Franz I Stephan of Lorraine. *Daily 10am–6pm | entrance fee 5 euros | Neuer Markt | www.kaisergruft.at | bus 3A, U1, U3 Stephansplatz*

22 KUNSTHISTORISCHES MUSEUM
★ ● (126 B5) *(🚇 J9)*

The 'Kunsthistorische', designed by the Ringstraße architects Gottfried Semper and Karl von Hasenauer, is one of the world's largest museums. Its holdings are the result of the collecting passion of Habsburg monarchs with a feeling for art who, starting in the 16th century, systematically amassed precious objects. The main attraction is the painting gallery

Alfred Hrdlicka's group of sculptures for the 'Monument against War and Fascism'

on the first floor. It is the fourth largest of its kind in the world. Its treasures include many major works by Bruegel, Rubens, Rembrandt, Dürer, Raphael, Titian, Tintoretto, Veronese, Caravaggio, Velázquez and other masters of the Italian, French, Spanish and Dutch/Flemish schools from the late 15th–17th centuries.

The collection's second focal point is the Kunstkammer (Collection of Sculpture and Decorative Arts) with priceless goldsmith work, carved stones and ivory, 'automatons', clocks, astrological instruments and much more. The magnificent paintings on the ceilings and walls by Ernst and Gustav Klimt, Michael Munkácsy, Hans Makart and others are also well worth seeing.

The magnificent building, opened towards the end of the 19th century, also houses a coin cabinet, the Egyptian and Near Eastern Collection, as well as a collection of Greek and Roman antiquities. On INSIDER**TIP** Thursday evening, an opulent buffet is served and there is a special tour with brunch every Sun *(reservations: tel. 5 25 24 40 25)*. The Collection of Ancient Music Instruments, the Collection of Arms and Armour, as well as the Ephesus Museum can be visited in the Neue Burg on the other side of the Ringstraße. *Main building Tue–Wed, Fri–Sun 10am–6pm, Thu 10am–9pm | entrance fee 12 euros | Burgring 5 | entrance Maria-Theresien-Platz | www. khm.at | tram D, 1, 2, bus 57A, U2 Babenbergerstraße, U3 Volkstheater, Neue Burg, Heldenplatz*

▉▉ LOOSHAUS (126 C3) (*Ɱ K8*)

No other architectural project in Vienna caused as much controversy as this residential and commercial building built by Adolf Loos in 1911. The bold design, with an elegant, unadorned exterior of green marble and glass, is a landmark on the path to the functional building style of the 20th century. *Michaelerplatz 3 | bus 2A, 3A, U3 Herrengasse*

24 MAHNMAL GEGEN KRIEG UND FASCHISMUS (126 C4–5) (*Ω K9*)

Since the 1980s, a monument by Alfred Hrdlicka on the square behind the opera house keeps alive the memory of victims of World War II and Nazi dictatorship in Austria. The group of sculptures incorporates the two-part, granite 'Gates of Violence', the bronze figure of the 'Kneeling Jew' and the marble statue 'Orpheus entering Hades'. The declaration of independence of the Second Republic of 27 April, 1945, is cited on a stele. *Albertinaplatz/Augustinerstraße | bus 3A, U1, U2, U4 Karlsplatz*

25 INSIDER TIP MARIA AM GESTADE (127 D2) (*Ω K7*)

The main attraction of this slender Gothic church (1343–1414), which once stood directly on the steep bank of an arm of the Danube, is the filigree 7-sided, helmet-shaped spire on top of its steeple. The bend in the axis between the nave and choir, as a result of the terrain, is an architecturally interesting element. The relics of St Clemens Maria Hofbauer, the patron saint of Vienna, are kept in a shrine in front of the altar in a side chapel. *Salvatorgasse/Passauer Platz | bus 1 A, 3 A*

26 MARIA-THERESIEN DENKMAL (126 B4–5) (*Ω J9*)

The enormous memorial between the Kunsthistorisches and Naturhistorisches museums, a work by Caspar Zumbusch (1874–81), shows Empress Maria Theresa surrounded by her comrades-in-arms for the good of the 'Casa Austria' – Generals Laudon, Daun, Khevenhüller and Traun on their horses, with her advisers Kaunitz, Haugwitz, Liechtenstein and van Swieten standing at her feet. *Maria-Theresien-Platz | tram D, 1, 2, bus 57A, U2 Museumsquartier, U3 Volkstheater*

27 MINORITENKIRCHE (126 B3) (*Ω K8*)

The three-naved hall Church of the Friars Minor, with ridge turrets typical of the

RELAX & ENJOY!

Visitors to Vienna can reach the meadows and hiking paths in the Vienna Woods and the – to a large extent, still natural – floodplains along the Danube by underground, bus and tram in less than half an hour. The *Alte Donau* **(130–131 C2–F4)** (*Ω O1–S7*) is especially close to the city centre and is a real idyll. This charmingly old-fashioned leisure area with beaches, boats for hire and cosy pubs was established on a waterway that was cut off from the main arm of the Danube around 140 years ago and is only 7 underground stations from St Stephen's Cathedral. Starting in April or May, several beach bars set up rows of deckchairs and serve cool drinks on the banks of the Danube Canal directly in the city centre. The top addresses: ● Strandbar *Herrmann* opposite Urania, at the mouth of the Wien River (**(127 E2)** (*Ω M8*) | daily | www.strandbar-herrmann.at | U4 Schwedenplatz), Tel Aviv Beach (**(133 E3)** (*Ω L7*) | Obere Donaustraße 26 near Augartenbrücke | daily | www.tlvbeach. at | U2, U4 Schottenring) and the Badeschiff (**(133 F4)** (*Ω L8*) | Franz-Josefs-Kai near Schwedenbrücke | daily | www. badeschiff.at | U1, U4 Schwedenplatz).

mendicant order, was built in the Gothic period (14th century). The elaborate tracery of the windows and portal, the mosaic of the Last Supper – a copy of Leonardo da Vinci's fresco – are outstanding. *Minoritenplatz | U3 Herrengasse*

28 MOZARTHAUS (127 D–E3) (*L8*)

The master lived in the late-Rococo house – the only one of Mozart's many residences in Vienna to have been preserved – between 1784 and 1787, and the opera 'The Marriage of Figaro' was one of the major works composed here. The building has been entirely renovated and now houses a comprehensive overview of Wolfgang Amadeus Mozart's Viennese years. *Daily 10am–7pm | entrance fee 9 euros | Domgasse 5 | www.mozarthausvienna.at | U1, U3 Stephansplatz*

29 MUSEUM FÜR ANGEWANDTE KUNST – MAK (127 F3–4) (*M8*)

European arts and crafts from the Middle Ages to the present day: glass, ceramics, metal, furniture, porcelain, textiles, as well as Eastern Asian artefacts: the collection in the Museum of Applied Arts is not only extensive but also presented in very effectively. Highlights include objects from the Wiener Werkstätte and oriental carpets. In addition, there are regular, fascinating exhibitions of modern art. The museum building, designed by the architect Heinrich von Ferstel, with a richly decorated red-brick façade in the style of the Italian Renaissance, is also worth special attention. *Tue 10am–midnight, Wed–Sun 10am–6pm | entrance fee 7.90 euros* **INSIDER TIP** *(free on Sat) | Stubenring 5 | www.mak.at | tram 1, 2, bus 4A, 74A, U3 Stubentor*

30 MUSEUM FÜR VÖLKERKUNDE (126 B–C4) (*K9*)

Vienna's Museum of Ethnography is one of the most comprehensive in Europe. The main highlights are James Cook's collection from Oceania, bronze sculptures from Benin and 'Old Mexican' treasures including the famous so-called Feather Crown of Montezuma. The building is currently undergoing extensive renovation and only a small part of the collection will be on display for some years. There are also fascinating temporary exhibitions focussing on one subject. *Wed–Mon 10am–6pm | entrance fee 8 euros | Neue Burg | Heldenplatz | www.khm.at | tram 1, 2, D, 46, 49, bus 48A, 57A, U2, U3 Volkstheater*

31 MUSEUM OF YOUNG ART (126 C2) (*K8*)

This museum which moved into the Palais Schönborn in 2010 is devoted entirely to international art of the 21st century and, as such, is unique not only in Vienna. The early works of the post-'68 generation are exhibited in spacious rooms. All genres are included and works by up-and-coming

artists, as well as those who have already become household names, are on display. The long-term goal of the permanent and temporary exhibitions is to introduce a new audience to the art of our time. *Opening times vary; call beforehand to check: tel. 5 35 19 89 | entrance free | Renngasse 4 | www.moya-vienna.at | tram D, 1, U2 Schottentor, U3 Herrengasse*

32 NATURHISTORISCHES MUSEUM
(126 A–B4) (*[map] J9*)

From dinosaur skeletons to the world's largest collection of insects with more than 6 million specimens, from the Venus of Willendorf – a 26,000-year-old stone statuette – to meteorites, precious stones and a gigantic skull collection – the impressive building on the Ringstraße houses one of the largest natural-history collections in Europe. An additional attraction: ⚡ INSIDER TIP tours of the roof (also with dinner). *Thu–Mon 9am–6.30pm,*

Wed 9am–9pm | entrance fee 10 euros| roof tours Wed 6.30pm, Sun 4pm | info: tel. 52 17 70 | Burgring 7 | entrance Maria-Theresien-Platz | www.nhm-wien.ac.at | tram D, 1, 2, 46, 49, bus 48A, U3 Volkstheater

33 NEUES RATHAUS
(126 A2–3) (*[map] J8*)

The splendid neo-Gothic New Town Hall was constructed in 1872–73. This is where the Lord Mayor and the municipal and provincial governmental authorities have their offices. The interior – the arcaded courtyard, ceremonial staircase and enormous ceremonial hall – can be visited on a guided tour. The 6m (19ft)-high Rathausmann (Town Hall Man), a kind of gigantic iron mascot holding a standard, watches over the city from the top of the almost 100m (330ft)-high tower. In summer, opera and concert films are shown on an enormous screen in front of the main façade with its filigree loggias, balconies

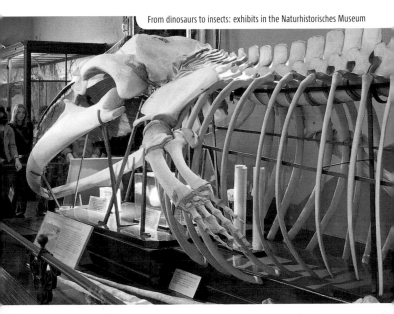

From dinosaurs to insects: exhibits in the Naturhistorisches Museum

Plague Column: Baroque tower of clouds

and lancet windows. There are also many monuments in the Rathauspark. *Friedrich-Schmidt-Platz 1 | free tours Mon, Wed and Fri 1pm (except when in session or on holidays) | tel. 5 25 50 | tram 1 Rathausplatz, U2 Rathaus*

34 ÖSTERREICHISCHES THEATER-MUSEUM (126 C4) (*∅ K9*)

The 1.5 million objects make the Austrian Theatre Museum in the magnificent Palais Lobkowitz the largest of its kind in the world. There are also regular special exhibitions in its splendid Baroque halls. *Nov–April Tue–Sun 10am–6pm, May–Oct Tue–Sun 9.30am–6pm (tours by appointment) | tel. 5 25 24 34 60 | entrance fee 8 euros | Lobkowitzplatz 2 | www.theatermuseum. at | U1, U2, U4 Karlsplatz/Oper*

35 PALAIS FERSTEL (126 C2–3) (*∅ K8*)

This showpiece of Ringstraße architecture was erected for the National Bank by Heinrich von Ferstel in the years between 1865 and 1870. It was also the home of the Stock Exchange until 1877. Café Central, on the corner of Herrengasse and Strauchgasse, was famous as a meeting place for men-of-letters at around the turn of the 20th century. After years of being allowed to decay, the gigantic building complex, with entrances on three sides, and its shopping arcades, was finally restored in the 1980s. *Freyung 2/ Herrengasse 17 | bus 1A, 2A, U3 Herrengasse*

36 PARLAMENT (126 A3–4) (*∅ J8*)

The Parliament Building, erected between 1873 and 1883, is the seat of both the National and Federal Councils. The architect, Theophil Hansen, wanted the Greek ideals of democracy to be preserved through his choice of a classical style and the statue of the goddess of wisdom, Pallas Athene, in front of the main ramp. You can find out all about the history of the Republic, free of charge, in the visitors' centre (entrance, under the ramp). *Tours, except when in session and on holidays: Mon–Thu 11am, 2pm, 3pm, 4pm, Fri, Sat also at 1pm, mid-July–mid-Sept Mon–Sat also at noon and 1pm | bookings for groups: tel. 4 01 10 24 00 | entrance fee 4 euros | www.parlament.gv.at | tram D, 1, 2, 49 Stadiongasse/Parlament*

37 PESTSÄULE (127 D3) (*∅ K8*)

This Holy Trinity column was donated by Emperor Leopold I in memory of the plague that carried off more than 100,000 Viennese in 1679. The Baroque tower of clouds was designed by the theatre engineer Lodovico Burnacini; the base, by Johann Bernhard Fischer von Erlach and the sculptures, by Paul Strudel. *Graben | bus 2A, 3A, U1, U3 Stephansplatz*

38 PETERSKIRCHE (127 D3) (*M K8*)

St Peter's Church, built in the first half of the 18th century to plans by Gabriel Montini and Johann Lukas von Hildebrandt, is one of the most magnificent works of Austrian Baroque architecture. The main attraction in the interior is the fresco in the cupola by Johann M. Rottmayr: 'The Assumption'. *Petersplatz | bus 2A, 3A Peterskirche, U1, U3 Stephansplatz*

39 POSTSPARKASSE (127 F3) (*M L8*)

The great innovator Otto Wagner, who always championed the unity of functionality and beauty and whose buildings have marked Vienna's appearance, created one of the pioneering feats of modern architecture and his own personal masterpiece with the understated elegance of the Postal Savings Bank. Not only the exterior, faced with sheets of marble and granite and crowned with two aluminium guardian angels, is worth seeing; the glass-roofed main hall where the interior decoration was planned to perfection down to the tiniest detail by Otto Wagner himself, is another landmark in modern architecture. *Georg-Coch-Platz 2 | tram 2 Julius-Raab-Platz*

40 RINGSTRASSE ★

(126–127 B–F 1–5) (*M J–M7–9*)

After Emperor Franz Joseph had ordered that Vienna's old defence walls be torn down in 1857, he had a splendid boulevard created to take their place. It circles the historical city centre and meets the Danube Canal at two places on Franz-Josefs-Kai. This 4.5km (3mi)-long ring road is lined by numerous majestic private and public buildings in what is known as the 'Ringstraße Style'. They all imitate that of earlier eras from Greco-Roman Antiquity, Gothic cathedrals, the Renaissance and Baroque, to Historicism as a mixture of all possible genres. A work of art in its entirety, the 'Ring' was opened in 1865. No other European metropolis has anything to match it. Pedestrians have to share certain sections of the Ringstraße with cyclists.

41 RUPRECHTSKIRCHE

(127 D2) (*M L7–8*)

The oldest, preserved church in Vienna. It is said that St Ruprecht's was founded around 740AD. Its nave and the lower section of the tower are Romanesque from the early 12th century. *Ruprechtsplatz | bus 2A, U1, U4 Schwedenplatz*

KEEP FIT!

A visit to the recently completely modernised ● *Therme Wien (Vienna Spa)* **(143 D4) (*M O*)** will refresh both your body and soul. Saunas and aroma grottos, gyms, beauty salons and above all the spacious pool landscape ensure that here, in Oberlaa on the south-eastern outskirts of Vienna, you will feel good all over *(Kurbadstraße 14 | Mon–Sat 9am–10pm, Sun, holidays 8am–10pm | entrance fee 15–22 euros (depending on length of stay) | tel. 6 80 09 | www.thermewien.at | U1 Reumannplatz, then tram 67 Therme Wien).*

The Hauptallee in the Prater and the paths on the Danube Island, as well as in the Stadtpark, Türkenschanzpark and Schönbrunn Palace Park are especially popular with joggers and Nordic walkers. More information on running courses under: *www.runningcheckpoint.at.*

42 SCHATZKAMMER ★

(126 C4) (*⊞ K8*)

The Imperial Treasury, one of the world's most valuable collections of religious and secular artefacts, is located in the oldest section of the Hofburg, the Schweizerhof. You will be dazzled by the priceless coronation insignia and order ornamental pieces, nation emblems, jewellery and mementos displayed in the 20 rooms. The 'Imperial Regalia' and relics of the Holy Roman Empire of the German Nation are among the most precious objects. These include the orb and sword, sceptre, the legendary holy lance that supposedly pierced the breast of Jesus Christ, as well as the Crown of the Reich, created in 962AD, making it the oldest of its kind in the world. The

Eager to learn: white Lipizzaner horses in the Spanish Riding School

treasure that Maria of Burgundy brought into her marriage with the later Emperor Maximilian I in 1477 are similarly precious, as are those of the Order of the Golden Fleece. Many weird and wonderful items can be seen in Ferdinand I's Kunstkammer (Cabinet of Curiosities). *May–Oct Wed–Mon 9.30am–6pm, Nov–April Wed–Mon 10am–6pm | entrance fee 12 euros | Hofburg/Schweizerhof | www.khm.at | tram D, 1, 2, bus 2A, 57 A Burgring*

43 SECESSION (126 C6) (*⊞ K9*)

In 1897/98, Josef Maria Olbrich created this exhibition and club building for the 'Viennese Secession', a group of avant-garde artists who split from their conservative colleagues. The latter had their headquarters in the Künstlerhaus. The Secession building, with a dome of filigree, gold-plated foliage – which was once ridiculed as looking like a 'head of cabbage' – is one of the principal works of Viennese Jugendstil. Gustav Klimt's *Beethoven Frieze* is displayed in the cellar. *Friedrichstraße 12 | Tue–Sun and holidays 10am–6pm | entrance fee 8.50 euros, 5 euros for exhibitions | www.secession.at | U1, U2, U4 Karlsplatz*

44 SPANISCHE HOFREITSCHULE

(126 C6) (*⊞ K8*)

One of the unusual things about Vienna is the fact that there are stables in the centre of the city, in the Imperial Palace itself, housing the Spanish Riding School with its Lipizzaner stallions. You can watch the white horses learning their paces at morning training *(Tue–Fri 10am–noon)*. Tickets, also for the tours including a visit to the stables lasting around one hour, are available at the visitors' centre *(Tue–Sun 9am–4pm, Fri on performance days 9am–7pm | ticket 16 euros, combined ticket with tour: 26 euros)*. Tickets for the much less frequent gala performances can be booked by post *(Hofburg | Michaelerplatz 1 | A-1010 Wien)* or under *www.srs.at.* Performance info: *tel. 5 33 90 31*

45 STAATSOPER (126 C5) (*K9*)

The Imperial and Royal Opera House, with its loggia, arcades on the side and metal barrel roof, was subjected to massive criticism when inaugurated in 1869. In the meantime, the Viennese have come to admire the romantic-historicising building which was severely damaged in the final weeks of World War II in 1945, and consider it one of the main symbols of the city's musical culture. The interior, with the frescoed staircase, Schwind Foyer, the Gustav Mahler and Marble Halls, and auditorium accommodating 2276, can be visited on a guided tour *(times at the side entrance or tel. 5 14 44 26 13).*

The INSIDER**TIP** *Staatsopernmuseum* provides an extensive overview of the opera house's history and present-day activities. *(Tue–Sun 10am–6pm | entrance: Goethegasse/Hanuschhof 1). Opernring 2 | tram D, 1, 2, bus 59A, U1, U2, U4 Karlsplatz/Oper*

46 STADTPARK
(127 E–F 4–5) (*L–M 8–9*)

This green island of tranquillity was opened in 1862 and was the first park to be established by the city administration. Its serpentine paths are lined with monuments. The most famous shows Johann Strauss Jr. getting his orchestra ready to perform a waltz. The beautiful stairways and pavilions next to the Stadtpark underground station – designed by the Jugendstil architect Friedrich Ohmann – have been painstakingly renovated. *Parkring | tram 1, 2, U4 Stadtpark, U3 Stubentor*

47 STEPHANSDOM ★ ●
(127 D3) (*L8*)

St Stephen's Cathedral, which the Viennese lovingly call 'Steffl', is one of the city's main

Austria's biggest bell, the 'Pummerin', in St Stephen's Cathedral

landmarks and Austria's most important example of Gothic architecture. Its history can be traced back to 1147 when the first Romanesque church was consecrated here. This was replaced in the middle of the 13th century by another Romanesque building whose remains – the Giant's Door (Riesentor) and two Heathen Towers (Heidentürme) – still form the western front of the cathedral.

The building as we know it today was created in several stages: 1303–40, the three-naved Albertine Choir; starting in 1359, the main nave with its magnificent stellar and net rib vaulted ceilings, as well as the 137m (450ft)-high south tower. Its planned companion piece, the north tower, was never completed and was adorned with a small, Renaissance-style dome in 1579 where the Pummerin, a 44,380lb bell made from the metal of canons captured during the second Turkish siege (1683), now hangs.

The interior of the cathedral, which the architect Adolf Loos described as the 'most

The arcades of the University are decorated with the busts of 154 famous scientists

solemn on earth', houses numerous unique artistic treasures. The most important are the pulpit made by Anton Pilgram in 1514/15, the Gothic 'Wiener Neustadt Altar' from 1447, the cenotaph of Emperor Friedrich III which Niclas Gerhaert van Leyden worked on from 1467–1513, and the tomb of Prince Eugene of Savoy from 1754. It is also worth visiting the catacombs where the mortal remains of 15 early Habsburgs rest in peace, as well as the organs of another 56 members of the dynasty preserved in urns while their bodies are buried in the Imperial Vault. If you manage to climb up the 343 narrow steps to the ☃ INSIDER TIP Tower Keeper's Room in the south tower, you will be rewarded with a fairy-tale view over the city.

You should also take a closer look at the *Haas House* opposite the cathedral. At the time it was opened in the 1970s, this building with its glass façade designed by the star architect Hans Hollein, was the subject of much criticism. Today it houses a hotel and several shops.

Cathedral tours Mon–Sat 10.30am and 3pm, Sun and holidays only 3pm | entrance fee 4.50 euros | evening tours with a visit to the roof June–Sep Sat approx. 7pm | tickets 10 euros | catacombs (only with tour) entrance fee 4.50 euros | Mon–Sat 10am–11.30am and 1.30pm–4.30pm, Sun and holidays only in the afternoon, every half hour; ascent of the south tower daily 9am–5.30pm | entrance fee 3.50 euros | lift to the Pummerin bell in the north tower July/Aug daily 8.15am–6pm, Sep–June 8.15am–4.30 pm | entrance fee 4.50 euros | all-inclusive ticket with audio-guide, one adult, one child 14.50 euros | Stephansplatz | www.stephanskirche.at | U1, U3 Stephansplatz

48 UNIVERSITY (126 B2) (ぬ J7)

The main building of the University of Vienna, which was founded in 1365, is one of the most spectacular buildings on the Ringstraße. It was built in the neo-Renaissance style to plans drawn up by Heinrich Ferstel in the 1870s and can be toured with an audio-guide. The highlight of the exceedingly interesting tour is the series of busts of 154 famous scientists in the arcaded courtyard. *Audio-guide from the porter, Mon–Fri 9am–4pm | fee: 3 euros (ID required!) | tours Thu 6pm, Sat 10.30am | entrance fee 5 euros | Dr.-Karl-Lueger-Ring 1 | event.univie.ac.at | U2, U3 Schottentor*

49 VOLKSGARTEN
(126 B3–4) (*Ø J–K8*)

After Napoleon had had the castle bastions torn down, a park, with a strictly geometric layout, was laid out 'for the people' on the space created. Peter Nobile erected the Theseus Temple in the middle of the complex. The rose garden near the exit to the Burgtheater is famous for its splendid blossoms. *Tram D, 1, 2, 46, 49, bus 2A, 48A*

WESTERN SUBURBS

With the opening of the Museums-Quartier – the MQ – at the latest, the Seventh District 'Neubau' developed into a hotspot for art freaks and trend scouts. Even before that, the once depressing INSIDER TIP Gürtel and its western border had metamorphosed into a chic cultural and gastronomic area. Fashionable bars and restaurants, boutiques and way-out arts and crafts shops are shooting up like mushrooms in the streets in between. The charming Biedermeier Spittelberg district is a model of idyllic urban life.

The neighbouring Josefstadt district has long enjoyed a reputation as a culture zone – albeit a rather bourgeois one – mainly due to the theatre of the same name. Most of the architecture here, and in the ninth district to the north 'Alsergrund', dates from the 19th century

The New General Hospital (AKH), one of the largest complexes of its kind in Europe, is another landmark. The spacious grounds of the Old General Hospital nearby now function as a university campus and have done a great deal to rejuvenating the area.

1 INSIDER TIP JOSEPHINUM
(132 C2) (*Ø J6*)

The collection of the Institute for the History of Medicine documents the development of medical Vienna from Gerard van Swieten, the personal physician of Maria Theresa, to Sigmund Freud. The main attractions are the life-size anatomical wax figures that Emperor Joseph II had modelled in Florence in 1785 so that his

GREEN-AND-WHITE OR VIOLET

The traditional Viennese clubs – not to mention Austrian football in general – have been going through a lean period in recent years. This means that the hope of experiencing great football is not the main reason for going to the stadium. It is much more the long club histories of the 'green-and-whites from Hütteldorf' and the 'violets' (Austria Vienna) that draw their supporters to matches. Enthusiasm and authentically Viennese atmosphere can always be guaranteed. *SK Rapid (142 C3) (Ø O) | Hanappi Stadium | 14th district | Keisslergasse 6 | tel. 5 44 54 40 | www.skrapid.at | U4 Hütteldorf; FK Austria (143 D4) (Ø O) | Horr Stadium | 10th district, Fischhofgasse 14 | tel. 6 88 01 50 | www.fk-austria.at | U1 Reumannplatz, from there bus 15A or tram 67*

military doctors would have the possibility to study the insides of the human body. *Mon–Sat 10am–6pm | entrance fee 2 euros | Währinger Straße 25/1 | tram 37, 38, 40–42 Sensengasse*

■2 LIECHTENSTEIN MUSEUM
(132–133 C–D2) (*ω J6*)

The collections of the Princely House of Liechtenstein are considered the most important and largest in private ownership in the world. Among its most valuable exhibits are pictures by Cranach, Raphael and Rembrandt, as well as several major works by Peter Paul Rubens. In addition, superb statues, weapons, porcelain and many other objets d'art are on display. These treasures are all shown in the Baroque palace of the Liechtenstein family, who have played a very influential role in the Habsburg realm for centuries, that

was renovated at great cost and with exquisite taste. *Currently, the collection can only be visited as part of a tour on certain Fridays at 3pm | bookings required: tel. 319 57 67-153 | entrance fee 20 euros | www.liechtensteinmuseum.at | Fürstengasse 1 | tram D Seegasse*

■3 MUSEUMSQUARTIER ★
(126 A–B 4–5) (*ω J9*)

In 2001, a unique museum complex was opened on the 15 acre site of the former Court Stables after a thorough redevelopment of the area. Together with the Kunsthistorisches Museum and Museum of Natural History on the other side of Museumsplatz, one of the largest artistic districts in the world was created. More than 20 museums, autonomous initiatives and projects have been established here and make the MuseumsQuartier – or

Super comfort and super art: a creative break in the MQ's inner courtyard

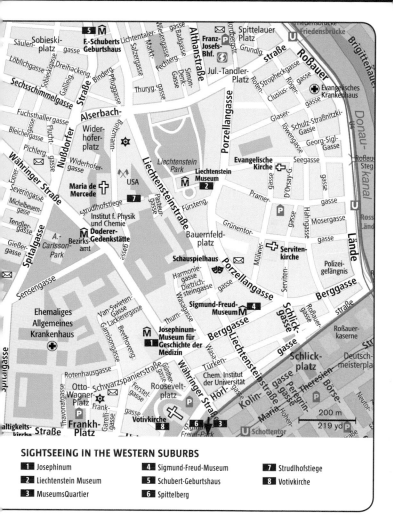

SIGHTSEEING IN THE WESTERN SUBURBS

- **1** Josephinum
- **2** Liechtenstein Museum
- **3** MuseumsQuartier
- **4** Sigmund-Freud-Museum
- **5** Schubert-Geburtshaus
- **6** Spittelberg
- **7** Strudlhofstiege
- **8** Votivkirche

'MQ' for short – both an artistic laboratory and place for experimentation and theoretical reflection, as well as a location where art is produced and presented. Gigantic lounges in the inner courtyard invite visitors to muse, chat and relax. The *Leopold Museum* – with the world's largest collection of works by Egon Schiele as well as masterpieces by Gustav Klimt, Oskar Kokoschka, Herbert Boeckl, Alfred Kubin and many others – is one of the most important institutions in the MQ *(Wed–Mon 10am–6pm, Thu 10am–9pm/ entrance fee 11 euros)*. Another is the *Museum Moderner Kunst (Museum of Modern Art)* with collections of classical

No cars here: cosy restaurants in the Spittelberg district

perimental spaces in the fields of film, new media and art theory called *Quartier 21*. With its ten entrances and exits and numerous cafés and restaurants, the MQ is an attractive stop between the city centre and the neighbouring districts and pulsates with life until late at night. *Museumsplatz 1 | tel. 523 58 81 | www. mqw.at | tram 49, bus 2A, 48A, U2, U3 Volkstheater or Museumsquartier*

4 SIGMUND FREUD MUSEUM ●
(133 D2) *(ØJ–K 6)*

Manuscripts and other memorabilia are displayed in the rooms where the father of psychoanalysis had his offices until he was forced to leave Austria in 1938. The famous couch, however, is not among the exhibits. *Oct–June daily 9am–5pm, July–Sep daily 9am–6pm | entrance fee 7 euros | Berggasse 19 | tram D, 37, 38, 40–42, bus 40A Berggasse*

5 SCHUBERT-GEBURTSHAUS
(128 C6) *(ØJ5)*

The prince of song, Franz Schubert, first saw the light of day in this typical Old-Viennese suburban house on 31 January, 1797. A room dedicated to the writer Adalbert Stifter is also attached to the museum. *Tue–Sun 10am–1pm and 2–6pm | entrance fee 2 euros | Nussdorfer Straße 54 | tram 37, 38 Canisiusgasse*

6 SPITTELBERG (126 A5) *(ØJ9)*

Visitors will be charmed by the picturesque suburban atmosphere of these narrow, car-free, streets with their small shops and cosy inns. The area between Siebensterngasse and Burggasse, Kirchberggasse and Stiftgasse, directly behind the Museums-Quartier, was built just before and during the Biedermeier period. It has the careful redevelopment carried out in the 1970s to thank for its present day popularity. *Tram 49, bus 48A, U3 Volkstheater*

modern art, the Austrian avant-garde of the post-war years and the most important contemporary movements such as Informel, Photorealism, Ready-made and Performance Art *(Fri–Wed 10am–6pm, Thu 10am–9pm| entrance fee 9 euros).* The same area also houses the headquarters of the *Kunsthalle (daily 10am–7pm, Thu 10am–9pm | entrance fee 7euros)*, the *Architekturzentrum Wien*, the *Tanzquartier Wien*, the *Zoom Kindermuseum* together with the *Jungle Theatre (various performance times | entrance fee 3–5 euros)* as well as several halls for events and ex-

7 INSIDER TIP STRUDLHOFSTIEGE
(132 C2) (*J6*)

This elegant flight of steps which climbs the slope between Währinger Straße and Palais Liechtenstein, achieved literary fame in a novel by Heimito von Doderer. Doderer describes the exquisite construction decorated with wrought-iron Jugendstil lanterns created in 1910 to plans drawn up by Johann Theodor Jäger as 'the terrace-like stage of the drama of life.' *Strudlhofgasse | near Liechtensteinstraße | tram D, bus 40A Bauernfeldplatz*

8 VOTIVKIRCHE (126 A–B1) (*J7*)

After the young Emperor Franz Joseph I survived an assassination attempt in 1853, his brother Archduke Ferdinand Max initiated the construction of an atonement church. The result was a massive building in the French Gothic cathedral style designed by Heinrich von Ferstel. Consecrated in 1879, it is one of the major works of pure Historicism. *Rooseveltplatz | tram D, 1, 37, 38, 40–44, U2 Schottentor*

MARIAHILF, MARGARETEN & WIEDEN

This is one of the trendiest areas of Vienna: on both sides of the Wien River, near the flea market and Naschmarkt.

The narrow – and often quite steep – streets in the Sixth District 'Mariahilf' are lined with artists' cafés, trendy bars and unconventional shops. The same applies to the two neighbouring districts to the south, especially the area between Pilgram and Kettenbrückengasse as well as the Freihausviertel to the east. A stroll through the Naschmarkt, 'the belly of Vienna', is something like a pilgrimage for the senses. Mainstream shoppers will feel that they are in an eldorado on Mariahilferstraße, the street of shops with the greatest variety in Vienna. There are however not many sightseeing highlights. The Jugendstil

SIGHTSEEING IN MARIAHILF, MARGARETEN & WIEDEN

1 Dritter-Mann-Museum
2 Freihausviertel
3 Hofmobiliendepot
   Möbel-Museum Wien
4 Karlskirche
5 Majolikahaus
6 Mariahilfer Straße
7 Wien Museum Karlsplatz

architect Otto Wagner designed two beautiful houses on the Linke Wienzeile. The Theater an der Wien, which is steeped in history, is just down the street and Karlsplatz is dominated by the Baroque church.

1 INSIDER**TIP** ▶ DRITTER-MANN-MUSEUM (139 D2) (*Ⓜ K10*)

Original memorabilia dealing with the classic film, *The Third Man*, that was shot in Vienna in 1948, along with background information on the post-war years in the Austrian capital. *Sat 2–6pm | entrance fee 7.50 euros | Pressgasse 25 | www.3mpc.net | U4 Kettenbrückengasse*

2 FREIHAUSVIERTEL
(139 D2) (*Ⓜ K10*)

An extremely trendy area has established itself around Schleifmühlgasse – with galleries and a number of chic cafés and restaurants and shops that are often open until late in the evening. *U4 Kettenbrückengasse, U1 Taubstummengasse*

3 INSIDER**TIP** ▶ HOFMOBILIENDEPOT MÖBEL-MUSEUM WIEN
(138 B2) (*Ⓜ H10*)

You will get a feeling of the living, dining and smoking culture of the Habsburgs, as well as Viennese furniture art from the 17th to 20th century, in the Imperial Furniture Collection that has been laid out with great attention to detail. The main focus is on the Biedermeier and Historicism periods. Highlights include the Empire style Egyptian Cabinet, a room honouring the maker of bent-wood furniture, Thonet, and regular special exhibitions. *Tue–Sun 10am–6pm | entrance fee 6.90 euros | Mariahilfer Straße 88 | entrance, Andreasgasse 7 | www.hofmobiliendepot.at | U3 Neubaugasse*

4 KARLSKIRCHE (127 D6) (*Ⓜ K–L 10*)

After the plague had wiped out more than 8000 Viennese in 1713, Emperor Karl VI

vowed to build a church dedicated to the saint who had once helped those suffering from the Black Death in Milan, St Charles Borromeo, if the horror were to end quickly. The votive building, one of the most magnificent creations of Johann Bernhard Fischer von Erlach and his son Joseph Emanuel, was consecrated in 1737 and is considered one of the greatest masterpieces of European Baroque architecture. Its enormous dome, now green with patina, and the two equally impressive triumphal columns flanking the central front in the form of an ancient temple not only served to glorify God but also stress the imperial Habsburgs' claim to power. The oval interior, decorated in pastel colours, is crowned with a monumental fresco by Johann Michael Rottmayr in the cupola. Visitors can get a close-up view of it from a 32m (100ft)-high platform that can be reached in a glazed lift. *Mon–Sat 9am–12.30pm and 1pm–6pm, Sun noon–5.45pm | entrance fee incl. lift 6 euros | Karlsplatz | www.karlskirche.at | tram D, U1, U2, U4 Karlsplatz/Oper*

5 MAJOLIKAHAUS (138 C2) (*Ⓜ J10*)

The block of flats created by Otto Wagner with a façade of weatherproof ceramic tiles decorated with ornaments of twining plants, is a feast for the eyes of all Jugendstil fans. The house on the corner to the right with its filigree golden decoration was also planned by Wagner. The medallions of women's heads were created by Kolo Moser, one of the co-founders of the Secession and Wiener Werkstätte. *Linke Wienzeile 38 and 40 | U4 Kettenbrückengasse*

6 MARIAHILFER STRASSE
(138 A–C 1–2) (*Ⓜ J–E 9–11*)

The section between the Westbahnhof and the MuseumsQuartier, in particular, with its attractive mix of department stores,

Mariahilfer Straße: popular place to shop for a wide variety of mainstream products

restaurants, bars and unusual shops, tempts many visitors. *Tram 52, 58, 6, 9, 18, bus 13A, 14A, 2A, U3 Zieglergasse and Neubaugasse, U3, U6 Westbahnhof*

■7 WIEN MUSEUM KARLSPLATZ
(127 D6) (*ĝ L10*)

Appearances can be deceptive. An extremely interesting collection showing the development of Vienna from a prehistoric settlement and Roman legions' camp and its position as the residence of the Babenbergs and Habsburgs to the present day, lies hidden inside the walls of an unsightly 1950s building next to Karlskirche. First-class paintings from the Biedermeier and Jugendstil periods, archaeological finds, the 'Turkish booty' from 1683, documents dealing with the Industrial Revolution and the real one in 1848, arts and crafts, and many more interesting objects are on display. *Tue–Sun 10am–6pm | entrance fee 6 euros | Karlsplatz | www.wienmuseum.at | tram D, U1, U2, U4 Karlsplatz/Oper*

LEOPOLD- STADT & LANDSTRASSE

A popular Viennese song celebrates spring 'when the flowers bloom again in the Prater' and that is really the season when young and old swarm out to go for a walk or do sport on the main road through the area, the Hauptallee, and in the woods.

The Giant Ferris Wheel is another major attraction with the Volks Prater (People's Prater) or Wurstelprater at its feet. Business people think highly of the modernised infrastructure of the neighbouring exhibition grounds. The labyrinth of streets between Nestroyplatz and Karmelitermarkt – until the onslaught of Nazi terror, the traditional home of Viennese Jews – has also become increasingly fashionable in recent years.

LEOPOLDSTADT & LANDSTRASSE

The Third District, known as Landstraße, on the other side of the Danube Canal is extremely varied. It shows its most impressive side in and around Belvedere. The adjacent residential and embassy area between the Arenberg and Modena Parks is also elegant before things become more down-to-earth near the Rochusmarkt and along Landstraßer Hauptstraße. There are many government offices closer to the city, as well as the Music University, the Konzerthaus and Akademietheater.

■1 BELVEDERE ★

(140 A2–3) (*L–M 10–11*)

Prince Eugene of Savoy's former summer palace is a must for every visitor to Vienna. The spacious complex with its two palaces is not only considered Johann Lukas von Hildebrandt's masterpiece but also one of the most magnificent of all Baroque designs.

The general and conqueror of the Turks had the Upper Belvedere built on a slightly elevated site with all of Vienna at its feet purely for representational purposes. The long, superbly proportioned building now houses a gallery for Austrian art in its preciously decorated rooms. The main focus is on local classics from the Biedermeier (Ferdinand Georg Waldmüller, Rudolf von Alt), late-Romantic and late 19th century periods (Leopold Kupelwieser, Hans Makart) to Jugendstil, Expressionism and post-war art (Egon Schiele, Oskar Kokoschka). In addition, major works of international art form part of the collection including paintings by Caspar David Friedrich, Claude Monet, Vincent van Gogh, Emil Nolde and Edvard Munch. The real crowd-puller however is Gustav Klimt and especially his painting *The Kiss*, one of the most important Jugendstil works. And there is even room for a Baroque collection and medieval masterpieces.

The 'noble knight' actually lived in the Lower Belvedere (1714–16), an only minimally less impressive building, that also

Baroque splendour: a stroll through the park between the Upper and Lower Belvedere

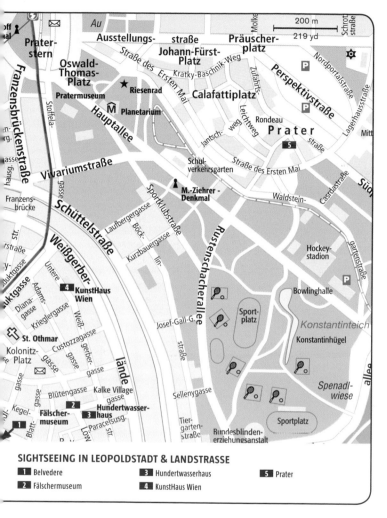

SIGHTSEEING IN LEOPOLDSTADT & LANDSTRASSE

1 Belvedere

2 Fälschermuseum

3 Hundertwasserhaus

4 KunstHaus Wien

5 Prater

has a marble hall lavishly decorated with frescos and stucco, a hall of mirrors and a state gallery. Temporary exhibitions of classical-modern or contemporary art are presented in the adjacent *Orangerie* and other artworks from the Middle Ages in the nearby state stables. The two palaces are linked by a garden more than 500 metres long that has now been returned to its original Baroque style. *Upper Belvedere daily 10am–6pm, Lower Belvedere Thu–Tue 10am–6pm, Wed 10am–9pm; Garden daily 6.30am–6pm, 9pm in summer | entrance fee Upper Belvedere 9.50 euros, Lower Belvedere 9.50 euros, combined ticket 14 euros | www.belvedere.at | Upper*

Wheel of fortune for ten minutes: the giant Ferris wheel in the Prater

Belvedere: Prinz-Eugen-Straße 27, Lower Belvedere: Rennweg 6 A | Upper Belvedere: tram D, Lower Belvedere: tram 71

■2 FÄLSCHERMUSEUM
(134 B5) (ω N8)

The Museum of Art Fakes is the only one of its kind in Europe. It offers fascinating background information on the criminal sides of painting and the art business. It also shows 60 fakes and copies of works by great masters. Very entertaining! *Tue–Sun 10am–5pm | entrance fee 4 euros | Löwengasse 28 | www.faelschermuseum.com | tram 1 Hetzgasse*

■3 HUNDERTWASSERHAUS
(134 B–C5) (ω N8)

This block of council flats is one of the creations of the artist Friedensreich Hundertwasser (initially in cooperation with the architect Joseph Krawina) that ignores all the rules of symmetry and right angles. Bushes and trees grow on the roofs and balconies, many of the walls and floors are curved and the façades are painted in all the colours of the rainbow. Out of consideration for the people living there, it is usually only possible to see the outside of the building *(Löwengasse/Kegelgasse | tram 1 Hetzgasse)*. However, Hundertwasser's *Toilet of Modern Art* in the *Kalke Village* shopping arcade *(Kegelgasse 37–39)* is open for public use. The artist's fans should also not miss out on visiting the Spittelau waste incineration plant **(129 D5)** *(ω J4)*, decorated by the master, next to the U6 underground station Spittelau.

■4 KUNSTHAUS WIEN
(134 B4) (ω N8)

This multicoloured museum has an exhibition space covering 38,000ft² and has a permanent display of Hundertwasser's work as well as temporary exhibitions of works by other well-known artists. *Daily*

10am–7pm, Sun and holidays tours at noon | entrance fee 9 euros; Mon 4.50 euros | Untere Weissgerberstraße 13 | www.kunst hauswien.com | tram 1, O Radetzkyplatz

5 PRATER ★
(134–135 B–F 3–6) (⌂ N–S 7–12)

The Viennese made this almost 15km (9½mi)-long landscaped area of woods and meadows with backwaters running through it their own as a recreation area after Emperor Joseph II had opened up the imperial hunting grounds to all in 1766. Today, the Prater is still one of the city's main 'green lungs' with cycle and foot-paths, tennis courts, a golf course, a trot-ting and racing track, and cycling and football stadiums.

A hotchpotch of amusement park and inns, the so-called Volks or Wurstelprater was established in the western section close to the city in the early 19th century. You can still feel something of its nostalgic charm in the old-fashioned ghost trains and the hall of mirrors, in the shooting galleries and beer gardens. In the mean-time, glittery gambling halls and hi-tech catapult rides have started to take over. The ten-minute ride on the Giant Ferris Wheel, the ☆ ● *Riesenrad* **(134 C3)** **(⌂ N7)**, is a must for all visitors to Vienna. This 67m (220ft)-high Viennese landmark constructed of iron was erected in 1896/97 and became world-famous when it was used as one of the settings in Carol Reed's post-war thriller *The Third Man (daily Nov–Feb 10am–7.45pm, March–April and Oct 10am–9.45pm, May–Sept 9am–11.45pm | 8.50 euros | www.wienerriesenrad.com).* The *Liliputbahn*, a 4km (2½mi)-long min-iature narrow-gauge railway has its station not far away. Next door, the *Planetarium* will take you on an excursion to the starry skies *(tel. 72 95 49 40). Würstelprater | www.prater.at | tram O, 5, suburban train 1, 3, 7, 15, U1 Praterstern*

IN OTHER DISTRICTS

BEETHOVEN MEMORIAL SITES

Ludwig van Beethoven changed his ad-dress in Vienna and surroundings approxi-mately 60 times. The two most famous places are the *Eroica House* where he composed his Third Symphony, the 'Eroica' in 1803/04 and the *Heiligenstädter Testament House*. That is where the musi-cian wrote his famous last will in 1802 in which he admitted to his fear of becoming deaf. *Eroica House* **(128 C4)** **(⌂ J3): by appointment only | tel. 5 05 87 47-8 51 73 | Döblinger Hauptstraße 92 | Testament House* **(129 D1)** **(⌂ J1): Tue–Sun 10am–1pm and 2–6pm | entrance fee 2 euros | Probusgasse 6 | both, tram 37, bus 38 A*

GRINZING ★
(128 A–C 1–2) (⌂ F–G 1–2)

There are many *Heurigen* districts – from Mauer on the southern border to Sievering, Heiligenstadt, Nussdorf and Pötzleinsdorf, and Jedlersdorf, Strebers-dorf and Stammersdorf on the other side of the Danube. But nowhere will you find more of these famous sanctuaries of Viennese *gemütlichkeit* in the classical style than in this wine-growing village on the north-eastern edge of the Vienna Woods that is now part of Vienna. How-ever, this also the place where most of the bus loads of tourists end up. Among the most popular addresses are: *Bach-Hengl (Sandgasse 7), Feuerwehr-Wagner (Grinzinger Straße 53)* and *Mayer am Pfarrplatz*. Wine grows on the slopes of Kahlenberg and Leopoldsberg and there are woods higher up – an eldorado for hikers and mountainbikers. *Grinzinger and Himmelstraße, Sand and Cobenzlgasse | tram 38, bus 38 A*

IN OTHER DISTRICTS

KARL MARX HOF
(129 D–E 1–2) (*M K 1–2*)

Fortress like blocks of council flats near the Danube Canal in Heiligenstadt are impressive witnesses to the heyday of 'Red Vienna' in the 1920s. The Karl Marx Hof is a classic example of this revolutionary kind of social housing with which the Social Democratic city council improved the miserable living conditions of the working classes. The complex, planned by Karl Ehn and built in 1927–30, contains 1600 residential units. *Heiligenstädter Straße 82–92/12.-Februar–Platz | tram D, bus 10A, 11A, 39A 12.-Februar-Platz, U4 Heiligenstadt*

NEUE DONAU (NEW DANUBE) ●
(130 A–C 1–6) (*M L–S 1–9*)

The artificial island almost 200m wide and many miles long between the main river and the excavated channel was created in the 1970s and '80s as part of extensive flood protection measures and was transformed into a gigantic recreation area (*www.donauinsel.at*). The ☀ *Donauturm (Danube Tower)* (131 D–E4) (*M P3*), erected together with the surrounding Donaupark for the International Garden Show in 1964, soars 252m (827ft) into the sky between the New and Old Danube, a little to the west of the UNO City. There is a wonderful view of Vienna from the revolving restaurant and it is also possible to bungee jump from its platform between April and October. *Bus 20 B Donauturm*

INSIDER TIP ► SANKT MARX
(139–140 C–D5) (*M D 1–2*)

Although surrounded by a busy urban motorway, Vienna's only Biedermeier cemetery to have survived in its original state is a paradise for the melancholic. A stroll through the park-like complex with its ivy-covered graves is a like a journey back in time to the early 19th century. A monument (*no. 179*) bears the name of Wolfgang Amadeus Mozart; however, it is still not certain where exactly he was buried on

BOOKS & FILMS

► **The Man without Qualities; The Strudelhof Steps** – Robert Musil and Heimito von Doderer scale literary peaks in their novels of the typical Viennese way of living and thinking in the years shortly before and after World War I.

► **Komm süsser Tod (Come Sweet Death)** – In his role as ex-detective Brenner, star satirist Josef Hader takes the audience to out-of-the-way snack bars, housing blocks on the periphery and the Danube Island Festival in Wolfgang Murnberger's criminal comedy.

► **The Third Man** – Director Carol Reed filmed Graham Greene's screenplay (the novella it was based on was published shortly after the film was released) in gloomy black-and-white in the clichéd greyness of post-war Vienna in 1948. In it, Orson Welles gets to know the ins and outs of the Viennese sewerage system.

► **Sisi** – Romanticists still go into raptures over Ernst Marischka's three Sisi films in which the young Romy Schneider moved audiences to tears in the 1950s with her portrayal of Empress Elisabeth.

6 December, 1791. *Daily June–Aug 7am–7pm, May and Sep 7am–6pm, Oct and April 7am–5pm, Nov–March 7am until nightfall | Leberstraße 6–8 | tram 71 Leberstraße*

SCHÖNBRUNN PALACE ★

(136 A–C 4–6) (*⟨⟩ D12*)

Along with St Stephen's Cathedral and Belvedere, the Habsburgs' summer residence – sometimes called Austria's Versailles – is Vienna's main attraction. In spite of all the splendour the complex does not seem to be at all flashy or pretentious but charming and approachable. It has its origins in an old bourgeois manor house that Emperor Maximilian II bought in 1559 and then expanded into a hunting lodge. After it was destroyed by the Turks in 1683, Johann Bernhard Fischer von Erlach planned the building in the basic form we see it today with two side wings, the spacious Court of Honour facing the street and the flight of steps on the garden front.

Schönbrunn finally became the focal point of the monarchy during the reign of Empress Maria Theresa who lived here with her husband Franz I Stephan of Lorraine and their 16 children. At her command, the young architect Nicolaus Pacassi remodelled the palace between 1744 and 1749 to adapt it to the late-Baroque taste of the time, added an additional storey as well as numerous balconies and staircases, created an impressive carriageway and built the charming Baroque Palace Theatre. The new, elegantly playful, Rococo style found its way into the residential and representative rooms.

Some 40 of the most beautiful rooms in the palace, from a total of more than 1400, can be visited on a guided tour. They include the Great Gallery, the Vieux Laque Room, the Millions Room with 260 Persian and Indian miniatures inserted into its

St Marx Cemetery: heaven for the melancholic

rosewood panelling, the Napoleon Room with the gigantic Brussels tapestries, the Chinese Round Room where Maria Theresa held her secret conferences, and Emperor Franz Joseph's spartan living and working rooms.

The Wagenburg (Carriage Museum), with its unique collection of 60 magnificent state carriages, is housed in a side wing to the west of the Court of Honour and there is a special children's museum in the main wing 'The Schloss Schönbrunn Experience'. On no account should you miss exploring the beautiful ● palace park.

It includes an enormous Palm House, a maze and Vienna's zoo. This architectural jewel from the Baroque period, founded in 1752, is considered to be the oldest existing menagerie in the world and even has a special 'Desert House' (opposite the Palm House in the park). The ☙ Gloriette, which crowns the top of a hill, supposedly recalls the victory over Prussia in a battle fought near Kolin in 1757. The graceful building was given new glazing some years ago to return it to its original state and now houses a café. To let your day at Schönbrunn come to a fitting close, you can listen to a concert in the Orangerie or go to an opera performance in the INSIDER TIP Marionettentheater or Palace Theatre, where occasionally operettas and plays are performed. *Palace park throughout the year daily from 6.30am–nightfall | Rooms daily April–June, Sep/Oct 8.30am–5pm, July/Aug 8.30am–6pm, Nov–March 8.30am–4.30pm | entrance fee Grand Tour (40 rooms) 13.50 euros, with tour 15.50 euros, Imperial Tour (22 rooms) 10.50 euros; Wagenburg April–Oct daily 9am–6pm, Nov–March Tue–Sun 10am–4pm | entrance fee 5 euros; Zoo daily Nov–Jan 9am–4.30pm, Feb 9am–5pm, March and Oct 9am–5.30pm, April 9am–6.30pm, May–Sept 9am–6.30pm | entrance fee 14 euros | www.zoovienna.at; Maze daily April–June and Sept 9am–6pm, July/Aug 9am–7pm, Oct 9am–5pm | entrance fee 3.50 euros; Palm House and Desert House daily May–Sept 9am–6pm, Oct–April 9am–5pm | entrance fee 4 and 2 euros respectively; combined ticket with Zoo 18 euros; Gloriette with observation terrace April–June and Sept daily 9am–6pm, July–Aug 9am–7pm, Oct 9am–5pm | entrance fee 2.50 euros; coffeehouse open throughout the year daily 9am–nightfall; concerts in the Orangerie throughout the year | tel. 8 12 50 04; Marionettentheater throughout the year | tel. 8 17 32 47 | www. marionettentheater.at; various combined tickets from Schönbrunn Classic Pass Light (16.50 euros) to Gold Pass (39.90 euros), including all attractions | www.schoen brunn.at | main entrance Schönbrunner Schlossstraße | tram 10, 58 | entrances also through: Hietzinger Tor, Hietzinger Hauptstraße, U4 Hietzing, Meidlinger Tor, Grünbergstraße, U4 Schönbrunn, and Hohenbergstraße, bus 8 A, 63A*

ZENTRALFRIEDHOF ●
(143 E4) (*Ø O*)

Since its opening in 1874, more than 3 million people have found their final resting place in the 600 acre central cemetery. The section with the graves of honour is especially noteworthy. Many great men and women are buried there – Franz Schubert, Johann Strauss, Beethoven and Brahms. Arthur Schnitzler and Karl Kraus were laid to rest in the spacious Jewish section with its special atmosphere. The Dr. Karl Lueger Memorial Church, a massive Secessionist work, can be reached from the main gate (Tor 2) and is well worth a visit. There is a precise plan of the cemetery at the main gate. *Nov–Feb 8am–5pm, March, April, Sept and Oct 7am–6pm, May–Aug 7am–7pm | Simmeringer Hauptstraße 232–244 | tram 71 | Zentralfriedhof 2. Tor*

THE GREAT OUTDOORS

INSIDER TIP DONAUAUEN
(143 F4) (*Ø O*)

A visit to the Danube floodplains near Stopfenreuth/Hainburg is an experience nature-lovers will never forget. This more than 35mi² large area of forest and wetlands was declared a national park in 1996 and includes one of the last largest untouched water meadows in Central Europe. You can explore it on (guided) tours, in a carriage or by canoe. The National Park Centre in Orth an der Donau acts of the 'gateway to the park'. *Mid-March–end of Sept daily 9am–6pm, Oct daily 9am–5pm | information and bookings: Mon–Fri 8am–1pm, tel. 02212 35 55 or www.donau auen.at | by car: from the city boundary,*

tion of it, the so-called Lainzer Tiergarten animal park, lies within the city limits. The Viennese use the last section of the Vienna Woods that has not been built on as a greenbelt recreation area. The 80km (50mi) of waymarked paths and several snack bars invite visitors to go on lengthy hikes *(mid-Feb–mid-Nov daily 8am–nightfall)*. You have a lovely view of the wood-

Deer in the Lainzer Tiergarten: a bit of countryside within the city boundary

Knoten Stadlau B3 via Gross-Enzersdorf to Orth; by mail bus: four times daily from Wien-Mitte to Orth and/or Stopfenreuth (travel time approx. 2 hours or 12 times daily from Südtirolerplatz to Hainburg (1 hour)

LAINZER TIERGARTEN
(142 B–C 3–4) (*ꚉ O*)

The Vienna Woods, extending over 483mi², surround the metropolis in a semi-circle on the west, and are the subject of songs, poems and waltz melodies. A 10mi² sec-

ed surroundings from the top of the ☼ Hubertuswarte. The *Hermesvilla (April–Oct Tue–Sun 10am–6pm, Nov–March Tue–Sun 10am–4.30 pm | entrance fee 5 euros | www.wienmuseum.at | U4 Hietzing, then tram 60, 62, and bus 60B from Hermesstraße stop)*, a hunting lodge in the Historicist style that Emperor Franz Joseph had built in 1882–86 and which is now used for interesting exhibitions as a branch of the Historisches Museum der Stadt Wien, is the most noteworthy attraction in the wildlife preserve.

FOOD & DRINK

Paris has its bistros, Madrid its bodegas, Prague its beer halls and London its pubs. But Vienna has three typical gastronomic institutions: the coffeehouse, *Beisl* and *Heuriger*.

Entire libraries are full of the literature that has been written about – and in – Viennese coffeehouses. In the Biedermeier period and even more around 1900, cafés were the focal point of Viennese intellectual life. Today, there are more than 500 such oases scattered throughout the city where you can sit for hours with a cup of *melange* and the obligatory glass of good Viennese mountain spring water without being bothered. They all have a wide selection of newspapers and many provide chessboards, bridge cards and even billiard tables to help you while away the time.

In Vienna, coffee is served in more than a dozen ways. This starts with the *grosse* and *kleine Schwarze* or *Mokka* (a small or large cup of black coffee) or *Braune* (the same, but with a little bit of milk). The *Melange* is served with a lot of milk and sometimes a little whipped cream, but always with a sprinkling of coffee, cinnamon or cocoa powder. The *Kaisermelange* is made even richer with an egg yolk. The *Fiaker* is a mokka served in a glass; the *Einspänner,* a Fiaker with a large amount of whipped cream. A cup of coffee thinned

'Bon appétit' and 'cheers!' the Viennese way: *BeisIn*, coffeehouses and *Heurigen* are doing better than ever

with water is called a *Verlängerter*. The classic 'Viennese Breakfast' is served in all coffeehouses. It consists of a pot of coffee (or tea) as well as bread rolls (called *Semmel* or *Gebäck*), butter, jam or honey, and a soft-boiled egg. During the day, most cafés also serve snacks such as sausages, toast, omelettes and goulash soup in addition to various types of cake. Many of the renowned cafés in the centre are also restaurants and some of them serve excellent food.

The second culinary stronghold of the Viennese way of life – the *Beisl* – has become trendy once again thanks to an amazing rejuvenation of the Viennese cuisine that is actually a mixture of Bohemian, Hungarian, Italian, Jewish and other Central European cooking traditions. For years, the city of schnitzel and

HEURIGEN

Viennese coffeehouse tradition –
here, in the Café Central

Tafelspitz (boiled beef), *Beuschel* (lights), *Knödel* (dumplings) and *Palatschinken* (pancakes) had a poor reputation with gourmets on account of the fat and calories. In the meantime, a new generation of ambitious cooks has adapted their menus to appeal to modern eating habits.

The third Viennese institution, the *Heuriger*, still enjoys tremendous popularity. Most of these inns have picturesque vaulted cellars, beautiful courtyards and gardens where guests are served young wine and hearty food – and often to live Viennese music. Most *Heuriger* are located in the old wine-growing areas on the edge of the Vienna Woods in the north-west of the city but those in the more peaceful districts such as Strebersdorf and Stammersdorf to the north across the Danube, or Mauer near the southern boundary of Vienna have just as much atmosphere. The genuine *Heuriger* – which is also known as a 'Buschenschank' – can be recognised by a fresh green fir branch over its door and a sign reading 'Ausg'steckt' next to it.

HEURIGEN

CHRIST (143 D2) (*Ⓜ O*)
His exquisite wines have made Rainer Christ one of the stars among Vienna's innovative, young wine-growers. His 400-year-old family operation is an idyll with a shady garden and bower, vinotheque and delicious buffet. *In odd months from 3pm, estate by appointment | Jedlersdorf, Amtsstraße 10–14 | tel. 2 92 51 52 | www. weingut-christ.at | bus 31A Haspingerplatz, tram 31 Grossjedlersdorf*

HERRMANN (142 C3) (*Ⓜ O*)
Lovely garden with vine arbour, inexpensive. *March–Nov Thu–Mon 3.30pm–11pm | Johann-Staud-Straße 51 | tel. 9 14 81 61 | www.weinbau-herrmann.com | bus 46B Härtlgasse*

REINPRECHT ●
(128 B1) (*Ⓜ G1*)
Renowned, spacious winery-cum-*Heuriger* in a former monastery, extensive buffet, large garden, live music every day. And Europe's largest collection of corkscrews. *Daily 3.30pm–midnight | Cobenzlgasse 22 | tel. 3 20 14 71 | www.Heurigerr-reinprecht. at | tram 38, bus 38A Grinzing*

SCHÜBEL-AUER (142 D2) (*Ⓜ O*)
The epitome of upper middle-class *Heurigen* culture with an excellent buffet,

garden shaded by chestnut trees and live Schrammel music; matinee concerts on Sat in June. *Tue–Sat 3.30pm–midnight | Kahlenberger Straße 22 | tel. 3 70 22 22 | www.schuebel-auer.at | tram D Beethovengang*

SIRBU ★ ● ☼
(143 D2) (*☉ O*)

Eat and drink at moderate prices in the midst of the vineyards with a panoramic view over Vienna. *Mid-April–mid-Oct Mon–Sat 3pm–midnight | Kahlenberger Straße 210 | tel. 3 20 59 28 | bus 38 A Armbrustergasse, then a long walk uphill, or by taxi*

COFFEE & TEA HOUSES

CAFÉ AMACORD (139 D2) (*☉ K10*)
Charming place to take a break between the Naschmarkt and Freihaus Quarter. Breakfast is served until 6pm; good cooking and moderate prices, large selection of magazines and games. *Sun–Wed 10am–1am, Thu–Sat 10am–2am | Rechte Wienzeile 15 | U4 Kettenbrückengasse*

CAFÉ CENTRAL ★ ● (126 C3) (*☉ K8*)
Luxurious café in Venetian neo-Gothic style. This is where men-of-letters and journalists sharpened their pens around 1900. *Mon–Sat 7.30am–10pm, Sun 10am–10pm | Herrengasse 14 | bus 1A, U3 Herrengasse*

INSIDER TIP FRAUENHUBER
(127 D4) (*☉ L9*)

Vienna's oldest café is a gem, with Persian carpets, red velvet and Biedermeier glass cabinets. *Mon–Sat 8am–midnight, Sun 10am–10pm, closed Sat evening in Aug | Himmelpfortgasse 6 | U1, U3 Stephansplatz*

HAAS & HAAS ★ ● (127 D3) (*☉ L8*)
This traditional tea house is famous for its many different types of breakfast. There is also a salesroom where you can buy exquisite teas and accessories. The inner courtyard with comfortable wicker chairs is a dream. *Mon–Fri 8am–8pm, Sat 8am–6.30pm, Sun 9am–6pm | Stephansplatz 4 | U1, U3 Stephansplatz*

MARCO POLO HIGHLIGHTS

★ **Sirbu**
Classic *Heuriger* with a panoramic view → p. 65

★ **Sperl**
Beautiful traditional coffeehouse → p. 67

★ **Café Central**
Splendid café that once inspired men-of-letters → p. 65

★ **Haas & Haas**
Exquisite tea house with a wonderful inner courtyard → p. 65

★ **Halle Café Restaurant**
Trendy, unpretentious and chic → p. 66

★ **Plachutta**
Tafelspitz and co: this is a stronghold of Vienna's boiled-beef tradition → p. 67

★ **Steirereck am Stadtpark**
Gourmet temple of the absolute highest quality on the banks of the Wien River → p. 66

★ **Gulashmuseum**
The paprika classic – served in 15 variations → p. 69

★ **Lusthaus**
Biedermeier-style dining – in the shade of chestnut trees in the heart of the Prater → p. 69

★ **Wrenkh**
Wholesome and good: heaven for hard-core vegetarians → p. 70

COFFEE & TEA HOUSES

HALLE CAFÉ RESTAURANT ★
(126 C6) (*∅ J9*)
Simple and chic, good food. In summer, there is a terrace with a view of the MQ courtyard. A place where the in-crowd meet with trendy exhibitions and special events in the house. *Daily 10am–2am | MQ, Museumsplatz 1 | U1, Karlsplatz U2, U3 Museumsquartier*

KORB (127 D3) (*∅ K8*)
Pleasantly laid-back café restaurant that is very popular with artists. Art Lounge in the cellar. *Mon–Sat 8am–midnight, Sun 11am–9pm | Brandstätte 9 | U1, U3 Stephansplatz*

LANDTMANN ☆ (126 B2) (*∅ J8*)
Large, classic – admittedly expensive – café on the Ringstraße, used by many politicians, journalists and businesspeople as a 'second office'. Delightful terrace. *Daily 7.30am–midnight | Dr.-Karl-Lueger-Ring 4 | tram 1, 2, 37, 38, 40–44, bus 1A, U2 Schottentor*

MEIEREI ☆ (127 F4) (*∅ M9*)
This 'milk bar' is part of the legendary gourmet temple *Steiereck* in the Stadtpark. It serves milk in all imaginable variations; 150 different types of cheese, schnitzel, healthy juices, the very best wines. Every

GOURMET RESTAURANTS

Coburg (127 E4) (*∅ L 8–9*)
Europe's largest wine cellar with the most variety is located under Palais Coburg. You can taste the good stuff in the bistro as part of a tour and dine magnificently in the gourmet restaurant. Tasting menu from 98 euros. *Daily 7am–midnight, restaurant Tue–Sat 6pm–10pm | Coburgbastei 4 | tel. 51818870 | www.palais-coburg.com | U3 Stubentor, U4 Stadtpark*

Le Loft ☆ (127 E–F2) (*∅ M7*)
You will relish all of the delights of France in this restaurant on the 18th floor of the fascinating Hotel Sofitel designed by Jean Nouvel: oyster tartare, frog legs, Breton lobster and scallop terrine. The almost 360° panoramic view through the windows over the roofs of the city will make you feel like you are in seventh heaven. Tasting menu from 73 euros. *Daily | Praterstraße 1 | tel. 9 06 16 | www.sofitel-vienna.com | U1, U4 Schwedenplatz*

Steirereck am Stadtpark ★
(127 F4) (*∅ M9*)
One of the world's best restaurants – the Steirereck ranked 11th on Restaurant Magazine's 2012 list – serves the highest quality international cuisine with a Viennese touch. Delicate small dishes are served in the ess.bar with the gourmet restaurant on the upper floor. Tasting menu from 55 euros at lunch; from 118 euros in the evening. *Mon–Fri 11.30am–2.30pm and from 6.30pm, ess.bar from 5pm | Am Heumarkt 2a | in the Stadtpark | tel. 713 3168 | www.steirereck.at | tram 1, 2, U4 Stadtpark*

Walter Bauer (127 E3) (*∅ L8*)
Intimate oasis for gourmets with seating for 30. Chef Tommy Möbius conjures up fine Viennese cuisine; Walter Bauer is responsible for the impeccable service. 5-course meal, around 79 euros. *Closed Sat, Sun; Mon evening only | Sonnenfelsgasse 17 | Tel. 5 12 98 71 | www.moebius.co.at | U1, U3 Stephansplatz*

hour on the hour: wonderful strudel straight out of the oven. Terrace with a view of the Wien River. *Mon–Fri 8am–11pm, Sat, Sun 9am–7pm | Am Heumarkt 2a | U4 Stadtpark, U3, U4 Landstraße*

SPERL ★ ● (133 D6) (*ω J9*)

'Old Vienna' to a tee: small marble tables, Thonet chairs and comfy booths, as well as billiard tables, a comprehensive selection of newspapers, fresh pastries and a faithful crowd of regulars; in short, a picture-book coffeehouse. *Mon–Sat 7am–11pm, Sun 11am–8pm, July/Aug closed Sun | Gumpendorfer Straße 11 | bus 57A Stiegengasse*

CAFÉ STEIN (126 B1) (*ω J7*)

The students' café with breakfast, good cooking and an Internet bar turns into a busy trendy tavern in the evening when Italian drinks and espressos become the order of the day. *Mon–Sat 7am–1am, Sun 9am–1am | Währinger Str. 6–8 | tram 37, 38, 40–44, U2 Schottentor*

RESTAURANTS: EXPENSIVE

HUTH (127 E5) (*ω L9*)

Elegant host and high-quality Viennese cuisine, fine wines, stylish living room in the cellar. *Daily | Schellinggasse 5 | tel. 513 56 44 | www.zum-huth.at | tram 2, D Schwarzenbergplatz*

MOTTO AM FLUSS (127 E2) (*ω L8*)

The new mooring place for the shuttle-boats to Bratislava lies like a luxurious yacht of glass at anchor on the right bank of the Danube Canal. In addition to a café and bar, it also houses a restaurant that became the in-place for the bourgeois, bohemian and business people in next to no time. Light, regional gourmet cuisine, fine wines, ☆ spacious terrace with a fabulous view of the canal; lavish breakfast served in the café until 4pm(!) *Daily |*

Stylish – *Sachertorte* in Café Sperl

Schwedenplatz | tel. 252 55 11 | www.motto.at | U1, U4 Schwedenplatz

PLACHUTTA ★ (127 E4) (*ω L8*)

Not only the *Tafelspitz* is top here. Ewald Plachutta and his team serve more than a dozen different kinds of boiled beef in their chic city eatery. *Daily | Wollzeile 38 | tel. 512 15 77 | www.plachutta.at | U3 Stubentor*

ZUM SCHWARZEN KAMEEL (126 C3) (*ω K8*)

The roots of this stylish classic restaurant can be traced back to the 17th century. Chef de cuisine Sevgi Hartl's cooking is creative while still respecting tradition

LOCAL SPECIALITIES

▶ **Apfelstrudel** – the dream desert made of grated or finely cut apples, nuts, and raisins, seasoned with cinnamon and sugar, wrapped in gossamer pastry
▶ **Beuschel** – finely cut offal (mainly heart and lung) in a spicy sauce
▶ **Buchteln** – Sweet yeast rolls filled with jam and often served with vanilla sauce
▶ **Frankfurter** – the sausages known as 'Wieners' everywhere else
▶ **Frittaten** – finely sliced pancakes served in clear beef soup
▶ **Kaiserschmarrrn** – desert made of shredded omelette, usually served with stewed plums
▶ **Nockerln** – the Austrian relative of Italian *gnocchi*; *Griess* or *Butternockerln* (small semolina or butter dumplings) are served in soup; *Salzburger Nockerln* – a soufflé of egg white – is a legendary desert

▶ **Palatschinken** – sweet pancakes filled with apricot jam, curd cheese, nuts or even ice cream (photo above left)
▶ **Powidltascherln** – Bohemian desert: paté choux filled with plum puree
▶ **Sachertorte** – the classic cake made of egg yolks, sugar, a little flour and beaten egg whites, filled with apricot jam and covered with chocolate icing
▶ **Stelze** – grilled knuckle of pork – side dishes: sauerkraut and bread dumplings – or veal, with more delicate accompaniments
▶ **Tafelspitz** – one of the best cuts of boiled beef; usually served with shredded fried potatoes and chive sauce or stewed apples with horseradish
▶ **Wiener Schnitzel** – the classic: escalope of veal covered with breadcrumbs and fried until golden brown; the perfect accompaniment: potato salad (photo above right)

and Maître Gensbichler guides his guests through the wine and cheese kingdom with the charm of times long past. The 'Camel' also has a stand-up bar and exquisite wine and delicatessen shop. *Closed Sun | Bognergasse 5 | tel. 5 33 81 25 | www. kameel.at | U3 Herrengasse*

RESTAURANTS: MODERATE

AUX GAZELLES (126 B5) (*𝝕 J9*)
The essence of the Orient for all the senses: the glamorous combination of brasserie, café and deli with an oyster bar, tea salon and club. It even has a Moroccan steam

bath! *Mon–Thu Café 11am–2am, Fri/Sat 11am–4am, restaurant Mon–Sat 6pm–midnight, club with DJ Thu–Sat 10pm–4am | Rahlgasse 5 | tel. 5 85 66 45 | www. auxgazelles.at | U2 Museumsquartier*

INSIDER TIP ZUM BLAUEN ESEL
(136 B4) (*C11*)

The ideal place for a meal after visiting Schönbrunn – don't be put off by the surroundings! Cosy restaurant with a wonderful garden with gravel underfoot and chestnut trees above. Excellent local cooking, steaks and scampi from the barbecue, and very good wines. *Closed lunchtime and Sun | Hadikgasse 40 | tel. 8 95 51 27 | www.blauer-esel.at | U4 Hietzing*

GMOAKELLER (133 F6) (*L9*)
Sophisticatedly refined home-style cooking using traditional recipes with a touch of Styria in the atmosphere of a cosy pub. Excellent wines. *Closed Sun | Am Heumarkt 25 | tel. 7 12 53 10 | www.gmoakeller.at | U4 Stadtpark*

GULASCHMUSEUM ★
(127 E3) (*L8*)

A different kind of 'museum' where 15 different varieties of the well-known Hungarian meat-and-paprika stew are served – you can sit outside in summer. *Daily | Schulerstraße 20 | tel. 5 12 10 17 | www.gulasch.at | U1 Stephansplatz*

HANSEN (126 C1) (*K7*)
Wonderful lunchtime restaurant in the cellar of the stock exchange with a view of lush green plants. Modern, light cuisine. *Closed Sat evening and Sun | Wipplingerstraße 34 | tel. 5 32 05 42 | www.hansen. co.at | tram1 Börse*

LUSTHAUS ★ ᝰ (143 E3) (*S11*)
Beautiful former imperial hunting lodge with terrace, gigantic chestnut trees and tangy wine. On balmy summer evenings, you will feel blissful here in the heart of the Prater woods. The kitchen will also satisfy sophisticated diners. *May–Sept Mon–Fri noon–11pm, Sat, Sun, holidays to 6pm, Oct–April closed Wed, Thu–Tue noon– 6pm | Freudenau 254 (Hauptallee) | tel. 7 28 95 65 | www.lusthaus-wien.at | bus 77A Lusthaus*

MARTINJAK (126 C5) (*K9*)
This comfy restaurant is designed as a mixture of a mountain hut and chic urban eating house and serves regional specialities from *Krautfleckerln* (baked cabbage and noodles) to *Blunzenroulade* (black pudding roulade). Popular place at lunchtime with a set meal at 7.80 euros; Fri chill-out with stone-pine schnapps and happy hour on Sat – both starting at 7pm. *Daily | Opernring 11 | tel. 53 56 96 | www. martinjak.com | U1, U2, U4 Karlsplatz*

NENI (132 B6) (*K10*)
Refreshing, aromatic Israeli-Levantine cuisine – *mezzeh*, *kibbeh* and salads. Café and charming rooftop restaurant; sandwiches to take away. *Closed Sun | Naschmarkt 510 | tel. 5 85 20 20 | www.neni.at | U1, U2, U4 Karlsplatz*

UBL (139 D2) (*K10*)
This is not the place if you are counting calories but perfect for fans of classic Austrian specialities such as schnitzel, knuckle of pork or fried offal served in a really relaxed inn with a round iron stove, old wooden panelling and floorboards. *Closed Mon/Tue | Pressgasse 26 | tel. 5 87 64 37 | U4 Kettenbrückengasse*

URANIA ᝰ (127 F2) (*M8*)
Chic combination of café, bar and restaurant with creative, international cooking. Terrace with a fantastic view of the Danube Canal (reserve!). Reasonably-priced set

meal at lunchtime. *Daily 9am–midnight | tel. 7 13 30 66 | www.barurania.com | tram 1, 2 Urania, U1, U4 Schwedenplatz*

WRENKH ★ (127 D3) (*ꭅ L8*)

Vienna's pioneer and master of healthy food is a Mecca for vegetarians. Fashionable with a chic bar, shop for 'functional food' and a 'cooking salon' with information on wholesome nutrition. *Closed Sun | Bauernmarkt 10 | tel. 5 33 15 26 | www.wrenkh.at | U1, U3 Stephansplatz*

LOW BUDGET

▶ A typically Viennese way – and one that is not at all expensive – to take the edge off your hunger until late at night is to have a snack at one of the sausage stands that can be found throughout the city. Some of the most popular ones are on Hoher Market and Albertinaplatz, Schwarzenbergplatz and Schwedenplatz.

▶ A whole range of international restaurants – Japanese, Turkish, Chinese, Persian and even Viennese – on the Naschmarkt **(139 D1–2)** (*ꭅ J–K 10*) serve good, inexpensive food.

▶ You can try authentic Turkish cuisine at *Kent*. Enormous selection, relaxed atmosphere, and unbeatable prices, lovely garden. **(132 A4)** (*ꭅ G7*) | *Daily 6am–2am(!), garden 9am–10pm | Brunnengasse 67 | tel. 4 05 91 73 | www.kent-restaurant.at | U6 Josefstädter Straße, tram 43* **(139 E2)** (*ꭅ F10*) | *second location daily 6am–midnight | tel. 7 89 80 38 | Märzstraße 39 | tram 9, 49, U3 Schweglerstraße*

CENTIMETER (126 A6) (*ꭅ J9*)

This local chain of restaurant is extremely good value for money. The menu in the form of a yardstick offers a great variety of gigantic, thickly-spread open black-bread sandwiches that you pay for by the centimetre. *Daily | Stiftgasse 4 | tel. 4 70 06 06 | www.centimeter.at | U3 Neubaugasse, tram 49 Stiftgasse*

INSIDER TIP ▶ CURRY INSEL (126 A3) (*ꭅ J8*)

Meat, fish and vegetable curries, served with coconut or lemon rice. Tamil culinary art of a high standard is served at low prices in this friendly restaurant. There is an all-you-can-eat buffet on the first Sat in the month (approx. 13 euros) and brunch is served 11am–3pm on Sun. *Daily, closed July/Aug. | Lenaugasse 4 | tel. 4 06 92 33 | www.curryinsel.at | U2 Rathaus*

GLACISBEISL (126 A5) (*ꭅ J9*)

This classic restaurant right behind the MuseumsQuartier serves good home-style cooking in post-modern surroundings. Inexpensive set lunch, wonderful garden. *Daily | Museumsplatz 1/entrance: Breite Gasse 4 | tel. 5 26 56 60 | www.glacisBeisl.at | U2, U3 Volkstheater*

INSIDER TIP ▶ INIGO (127 E3) (*ꭅ L8*)

Cheerful, laid-back meeting place for people from all walks of life. The vegetarian meals and set lunch for 5.90 euros are something special. *Closed Sun | Bäckerstraße 18 | tel. 5 12 74 51 | www.inigo.at | U3 Stubentor*

RAMIEN (126 B6) (*ꭅ J9*)

This pioneer among Vienna's modern Asian restaurants is highly praised for its unpretentious styling and wonderful cooking and has remained a favourite place for the city's young creative crowd. Fantastic noodle soups, rice dishes with tofu, duck, salmon and shrimps. *Closed Mon | Gumpendorfer Straße 9 | tel. 5 85 47 98 | www.ramien.at | U2, U4 Karlsplatz*

SCHWEIZERHAUS (134 C3) (*M O7*)

An institution in the Wurstelprater. Hearty old-Viennese specialities from schnitzel and silver carp to knuckle of pork and

9am–4pm | set meal from 11.30am | tel. 06 76 3 09 51 61 | U2 Museumsquartier, bus 2A Michaelerplatz

TIROLERGARTEN (136 B5) (*M C12*)

Hearty alpine cooking in a Tyrolean farmhouse – from bacon and bread, *Schlutzkrapfen* (noodles stuffed with spinach and curd cheese) and organic beef goulash to spinach or Tyrolean dumplings. In the even-

The Schweizerhaus – an endless stream of beer and hearty Viennese cooking

goulash. When the weather is fine, you can sit outside in the shade of enormous chestnut trees. *Mid-March–end of Oct daily. | Prater 116 | tel. 7 28 01 52 13 | www.schweizerhaus.at | U1 Prater – Messe*

INSIDERTIP SOHO IN THE NATIONAL LIBRARY (126 C4) (*M K 8–9*)

A canteen for government employees in the style of s designer restaurant with bistro cuisine at cafeteria prices. Different set meals every day and snacks. *Am Josefsplatz 1/Neue Hofburg | entrance from Burggarten next to Butterfly House (Schmetterlingshaus) or behind the Palace Chapel (Burgkapelle) door on the left | Mon–Fri*

ing, restaurant on the first floor with high-quality food – and just-as-high prices. *Daily | Schlosspark Schönbrunn | tel. 8 79 35 56 20 | www.gasthaustirolergarten.at | U4 Hietzing, then bus 15A or 56B*

WALDVIERTLER HOF (138 C2–3) (*M J10*)

A typical country inn – in the heart of town! Substantial specialities from northern Lower Austria; friendly, speedy service, cosy, rustic atmosphere and a large garden with chestnut trees – reasonably priced set lunches. *Closed Sat/Sun | Schönbrunner Str. 20 | tel. 5 87 34 47 | www.waldviertlerhof.at | U4, bus 59A Kettenbrückengasse*

SHOPPING

CITY WHERE TO START?
Stephansdom (127 D3)
(*𝄞 L 8*): Vienna's central shopping area is located around the cathedral. The Graben and Kohlmarkt are lined with exquisite shops as are Rotenturm and Kärntner Straße. It is considerably less expensive on the Landstraßer Hauptstraße, Wiedner Hauptstraße, Favoritenstraße and especially Mariahilfer Straße. There are many interesting and unusual shops in the side streets in the city centre and the Naschmarkt.

The Danube metropolis is an expensive spot. This applies particularly to top-brand articles from the international accessory and fashion industry. Traditional local products include gold, silver and enamel work, furniture, fabrics, fine Jugendstil and Biedermeier-style glassware, and you should not forget old and new books, as well as anything to do with music.

Fabrics are always an appropriate souvenir and you will be able to purchase traditional costumes and loden clothing, made-to-measure suits and shoes, and especially the creations of the young fashion designers in the area around Lindengasse and Neubaugasse.

Photo: Antiques market

Antiques, traditional clothing, jewellery and fine china: Vienna is not cheap but it is a good place to find stylish souvenirs

If you are more interested in classical souvenirs, Augarten porcelain, petit-point tapestries and the legendary *Sachertorte* – or no-less-delicious *Imperialtorte* – are always a good choice. The time-honoured aristocratic shops that still proudly display the 'K. & K. Hof' or even 'Kammerlieferant' shield are really special and worth visiting if only to experience their somewhat antiquated atmosphere.

Things are much more down-to-earth and sensual at Vienna's almost two dozen food markets; the most interesting is the Naschmarkt and the flea market is held next to it every Saturday. Opening hours have become fairly liberal in Vienna: many shops do not close their doors until 7pm or 8pm during the week; however, shopping stops at 6pm – at the latest – on Saturday. Most shops are closed on Sunday

The Meinl Moor: reminiscent of colonial days

etc. made of horn. *Singerstraße 8 | U1, U3 Stephansplatz*

HORN
Exquisite accessories and leather travel goods, timelessly elegant and perfectly crafted. *Bräunerstraße 7 | U1, U3 Stephansplatz* (126 C3) (*M K8*) | *Mahlerstraße 5 | U1, U2, U4 Karlsplatz* (127 D5) (*M K9*)

RETTI (126 C3) (*M K8*)
Jewels, clocks, candles. The portal is one of the architect Hans Hollein's earliest works. *Kohlmarkt 10 | bus 2A, 3A, U3 Herrengasse*

SCHULLIN (126 C3) (*M K8*)
Contemporary, fashionable jewellery. The entrance designed by Hans Hollein is an added attraction. *Kohlmarkt 7 | bus 2A, 3A, U3 Herrengasse*

although some souvenir shops in the centre are open and you can buy groceries at selected shops at the railways stations.

INSIDER TIP ▶ SILBERBOUTIQUE (127 D4) (*M K8*)
Classic silversmith art and modern design: exclusive bowls, baskets, centrepieces, candelabras, cutlery and souvenirs. *Spiegelgasse 14 | U1, U2 Stephansplatz*

ACCESSORIES, JEWELLERY & HANDICRAFTS

ANNA STEIN (139 D2) (*M J 10*)
Unusual souvenirs and knick-knacks – from felt purses and art cards to Brazilian jewellery. The atmosphere of a salon with a pavement café is an extra. *Kettenbrückengasse 21 | www.anna-stein.com | U4 Kettenbrückengasse*

SKREIN (127 D4) (*M K8*)
A young team of excellent artistic jewellers present their own creations and those of renowned colleagues. Extremely innovative and individual. *Spiegelgasse 5 | U1, U3 Stephansplatz*

FREY WILLE
Elegant, decorative enamel jewellery with 24-carat gold decoration. *Lobkowitzplatz 1 | tram D, 1, 2, U1, U2, U4 Karlsplatz* (126 C4) (*M L 8*) | *Stephansplatz 5 | U1, U3 Stephansplatz* (126 C4) (*M K 9*)

WALTER WEISS (138 C1) (*M J9*)
Hundreds of hand-made hair and clothes brushes that will last forever. *Mariahilfer Straße 33 | bus 2A Königsklostergasse*

ANTIQUES & OLD BOOKS

HARTMANN (127 D4) (*M L 8*)
Hand-made eyeglasses with an international reputation. Also, combs, shoehorns,

CHRISTIAN NEBEHAY (127 D5) (*M L9*)
Books and art, mainly from the Jugendstil and Secession era. *Annagasse 18 | tram D, 1, 2, U1, U2, U4 Karlsplatz*

INLIBRIS GILHOFER NFG.
(126 A2) (*ᗡ J7*)

On of the top addresses for Austriaca, autographs, old prints, books. *Rathausstraße 19 | tram 1, U2 Schottentor*

KOVACEK (127 D4) (*ᗡ K8*)

This is place to look for premium-quality antique glassware. *Stallburggasse 2 | bus 3 A, U1, U3 Stephansplatz*

AUCTION HOUSES

DOROTHEUM ● (126 C4) (*ᗡ K 8*)

You can buy all kinds of furniture, fine china, books, jewellery, toys and curios at all price and quality levels in the more than 300-year-old elegant pawnshop – either at auction or in the 'free sales' section. Wandering through the building and poking around is always worthwhile. *Mon–Fri 10am–6pm, Sat 9am–5pm | Dorotheergasse 17 | auction dates: tel. 5156 00 | www.dorotheum.com | U1, U3 Stephansplatz*

DELICATESSEN, TEA & WINE

BABETTE'S (139 D2) (*ᗡ K10*)

Very pleasant mixture of international cookery books and exotic herbs and spices. Also cookery lessons and freshly-made soups and curries at lunchtime. *Schleifmühlgasse 17 | U4 Kettenbrückengasse*

INSIDER TIP ▶ BÖHLE (127 E4) (*ᗡ L8*)

This delicatessen which is steeped in history, has a phenomenal selection of wine and spirits. Freshly-prepared spreads and small portions of warm delicacies are sold to take away. *Wollzeile 30 | tram 1, 2 Luegerplatz, U3 Stubentor*

JULIUS MEINL AM GRABEN ★
(126 C3) (*ᗡ K8*)

The best delicatessen in town. In addition to the fabulous selection of fine foodstuffs, the three floors also have room for a restaurant and café, as well as a wine and sushi bar. *Graben 19 | www.meinlamgraben. at | bus 2A, 3A, U1, U3 Herrengasse*

★ **Julius Meinl am Graben**
Delicatessen with specialities from all over the world → p. 75

★ **Steffl**
A department store full of tradition; the top address for fashion and lifestyle → p. 76

★ **Vinissimo**
Fine tipples from all the wine-growing regions in Austria – can also be tasted on the spot → p. 76

★ **Trachten Tostmann**
Buy or hire traditional clothes to make you look like a real Austrian → p. 79

★ **Naschmarkt**
Bazaar atmosphere at Vienna's largest and most fascinating food market → p. 78

★ **Augarten**
Vienna's world-famous figures made of 'white gold' are produced by Europe's second-oldest manufacturer of fine china → p. 77

★ **Altmann & Kühne**
Heaven for those with a sweet tooth – beautifully packed as well → p. 79

MARCO POLO HIGHLIGHTS

SCHÖNBICHLER
(127 D3) *(ⅢⅢ L8)*
Vienna's best tea specialist has more than 100 varieties from all over the world – from noble classics to modern mixtures in cool aluminium tins. *Wollzeile 4 | bus 2 A, U1, U3 Stephansplatz*

VINISSIMO ★
(126 A6) *(ⅢⅢ H10)*
First-class wines from all regions of Austria can be sampled in the small bistro. *Mon–Sat 11am–11pm | Windmühlgasse 20 | bus 2A, 57A*

FILMS, GAMES, MUSIC

DOBLINGER (126 C4) *(ⅢⅢ K8)*
Traditional shop for new and old sheet music as well as specialist literature and recordings. *Dorotheergasse 10 | U1, U3 Stephansplatz*

LOW BUDGET

▶ Vienna's most fascinating collection of vintage clothes: this is where you will find all of the fashion highlights of the past eight decades – from grandma's bodices to cutting-edge hot pants. **(132 B5)** *(ⅢⅢ M8)* Humana Retro – Trend & Jugend | Lerchenfelder Straße 45/ corner of Neubaugasse | tram 46 Piaristengasse

▶ Every Sat, second-hand dealers set up their stands near the Kettenbrückengasse underground station **(139 C2)** *(ⅢⅢ J9)*. There, you can find everything imaginable as well as a book flea market. *6.30am–6pm, to nightfall in winter*

GAMES CENTER
(126 B6) *(ⅢⅢ J9)*
Games for children and adults: Vienna's largest selection of board games. *Theobaldgasse 20 | U2 Museumsquartier*

SATYR (127 D2) *(ⅢⅢ L7)*
Specialist shop with 5000 German and 20,000 English DVDs, as well as an enormous selection of books. *Vorlaufstraße 2 | tram 1, 2, U4 Schwedenplatz*

DEPARTMENT STORES & MALLS

GERNGROSS
(138 C1) *(ⅢⅢ H10)*
More than 180-year-old, five-storey, department store. *Mon–Wed 9.30–7pm, Thu/Fri 8pm, Sat 9.30–6pm | Mariahilfer Straße 38–48 | U3 Neubaugasse*

RINGSTRASSENGALERIEN
(127 D5) *(ⅢⅢ K–L 9)*
There are 70 shops in this stylish 100,000ft² shopping arcade. *Kärntner Ring 5–7 | tram D, 1, 2, 71, U1, U2, U4 Karlsplatz*

STEFFL ★
(127 D4) *(ⅢⅢ L8)*
This traditional shop concentrates on fashion and lifestyle – exquisite and expensive. *Mon–Wed 9.30–7pm, Thu/Fri to 8pm, Sat 9.30–6pm | Kärntner Straße 19 | U1, U3 Stephansplatz*

ARTS AND CRAFTS, DESIGN & FURNITURE

ARTUP (127 D3) *(ⅢⅢ L8)*
Gallery-shop with a zany mixture of accessories for the home, fashion and exclusive souvenirs, produced by up-and-coming local designers as unique examples or in small series. *Bauernmarkt 8 | U1, U3 Stephansplatz*

AUGARTEN ★

The filigree figures and china from Europe's second-oldest porcelain manufacturer are some of the most popular Viennese souvenirs. You can see how the articles are made in a 1-hour tour through the headquarters in Augarten Palace. *Tours Mon–*

INSIDER TIP ▶ HABARI (126 B6) (*🗺 J9*)

Top-quality accessories and table decorations, jewellery and textiles from sub-Saharan Africa. There are special exhibitions in the cellar – entrance free! *Theobaldgasse 16 | www.habari.at | U2 Museumsquartier*

At Lobmeyr all that glitters is glass: from precious crystal chandeliers to vases

Fri 10am | 12 euros | Obere Augartenstr. 1 (133 F1) (🗺 L6) | Salesrooms also at Stock-im-Eisen-Platz 3–4 | U1, U3 Stephansplatz (127 D3) (🗺 K8) | www.augarten.at

BACKHAUSEN (127 D4) (*🗺 L9*)

This interior-decoration shop carries exquisite fabric for furniture and curtains, designer furnishing, gifts and home accessories – the focus is on Jugendstil. *Schwarzenbergstraße 10 | U1, U2, U4 Karlsplatz*

CARL AUBÖCK (132 A5) (*🗺 G8*)

Stunning design from paperweights to key fobs from a traditional studio that has received many awards. *Bernardgasse 23 | U6 Thaliastraße*

KAROLINSKY / WOKA (127 D4) (*🗺 L8*)

Jugendstil and art-déco lamps made to designs by Josef Hoffmann, Adolf Loos, Kolo Moser and others. *Singerstraße 16 | U1, U3 Stephansplatz*

LOBMEYR (127 D4) (*🗺 K9*)

Exquisite crystal chandeliers, mirrors, glassware. The Glass Museum on the 2nd floor is well worth visiting – and is free of charge. *Kärntner Straße 26 | U1, U3 Stephansplatz*

MARIA STRANSKY (126 C4) (*🗺 K8*)

This small shop sells the finest petit-point work –as Viennese as it gets. *Hofburg-Passage 2 | U1, U3 Stephansplatz, U3 Herrengasse*

MARKET

NASCHMARKT ★ ●
(139 D1–2) (_M J–K 10_)

'Vienna's belly': the largest and most charming food market in the city exudes the cheerful, sensual atmosphere of a bazaar. A special note: the dealers from the Balkans and Turkey who praise their wares at the top of their voices – and even give free samples! *Between Kettenbrücken-*

DISASTER CLOTHING
(132 C6) (_M H10_)

This is the place for way-out hip designer fashion – mainly shirts for him and her. Clothes hire for special events. *Kirchengasse 19 | branch: Neubaugasse 7 | both: tram 49 Kirchengasse, U3 Neubaugasse*

FLO (139 D2) (_M K10_)
'Antiques with stitches' is the motto of Ingrid Raab's boutique for vintage clothes.

More than 500 yards long and a wonderful feast for all the senses: the Naschmarkt

gasse and Karlsplatz on the Wienzeile | Mon–Fri 6am–6.30pm, Sat 6am–5pm | U4 Kettenbrückengasse

FASHION

ATIL KOTOGLU (126 C3) (_M K8_)
A top designer from Istanbul who mixes oriental and western elements. Some Hollywood stars have started wearing his cosmopolitan creations. *Habsburgergasse 10 | U1, U3 Stephansplatz*

More than 5000 items from Charleston dresses to the New Look of the 1950s, as well as silk stockings, model hats, costume jewellery and much more. Film stars and trend scouts like to rummage around in this shop. *Schleifmühlgasse 15a | U4 Kettenbrückengasse*

FREITAG ☺
(132 B6) (_M H9_)

This Swiss company makes bags and rucksacks out of no-longer-needed truck tarpaulins, the handles are strips of safety belts and old bike tubes are used for the seams. 1600 models in all colours of the rainbow in the heart of Vienna's hippest shopping district. *Neubaugasse 26 | U3 Neubaugasse*

GUYS & DOLLS (127 D2) *(𝄞 K8)*

Chic – mostly sporty – designer fashion for young people and – hats, caps, gloves, eyeglasses, etc. *Schultergasse 2 | bus 2A, 3A Wipplingerstraße*

HENNY ABRAHAM (139 D2) *(𝄞 K10)*

Exquisite, unique articles brought together from the four corners of the globe: from saris and kimonos, kilims and quilts to mother-of-pearl cutlery and rice paper. *Schleifmühlgasse 13 | U4 Kettenbrückengasse*

HUMANIC (132 C6) *(𝄞 J9)*

The largest shoe shop in Europe has everything from beach sandals to trendy sneakers, from high heels to hand-made brogues – more than 100,000 pairs displayed on over 30,000ft². *Mariahilfer Straße 37–39 | U3 Neubaugasse*

LAMBERT HOFER

You can hire costumes and evening wear here. *Leilgebgasse 5 | tel. 40 86 66 | tram 6, 18, 62 Matzleinsdorfer Platz* (138 C4) *(𝄞 H12)* | *Margaretenstraße 25 | U4 Kettenbrückengasse* (139 D2) *(𝄞 K10)*

PARK (132 B6) *(𝄞 H9)*

Avant-garde fashion and 1980s cult wear, unusual accessories, international fashion magazines and exclusive furniture on two floors near Mariahilfer Straße. *Mondscheingasse 20 | U3 Neubaugasse*

SCHELLA KANN (127 D4) *(𝄞 L8)*

Extravagantly modern couture for women with a fuller figure, functional, straight-forward made of luxurious fabrics and – usually – in dazzling colours. *Singerstraße 14 | U1, U3 Stephansplatz*

TRACHTEN TOSTMANN ★
(126 B2) *(𝄞 K7)*

Genuine traditional clothing for all the family. Also for hire. *Schottengasse 3A | tram D, 1, U2 Schottentor*

SWEET THINGS

ALTMANN & KÜHNE ★
(127 C3) *(𝄞 K8)*

Bonbons and mini-chocolates delightfully boxed. *Graben 30 | bus 2 A, 3 A, U1, U3 Stephansplatz*

DEMEL (126 C3) *(𝄞 K8)*

Superior boxes of chocolates and cakes from the former confectioner to the Imperial Court. There is also a **INSIDER TIP** Marzipan Museum *(daily 11am–6pm)*. *Kohlmarkt 14 | www.demel.at | bus 2A, U3 Herrengasse*

MANNER SHOP
(127 D3) *(𝄞 L8)*

These classic nougat wafers in pink wrapping are sold fresh everyday in the flagship store. *Stephansplatz 7 | U1, U3 Stephansplatz*

SACHER
(126–127 C–D5) *(𝄞 K9)*

Here you can buy the world-famous cake to take home with you or have it shipped anywhere in the world. *Kärntner Straße 38 | tram D, 1, 2, U1, U2, U4 Karlsplatz*

SCHOKOLADENWERKSTATT
(127 D4) *(𝄞 L8)*

A small temple full of exquisite, wickedly tasty goodies for all compulsive nibblers and chocoholics. *Ballgasse 4 | www.schoko ladenwerkstatt.at | U1, U3 Stephansplatz*

ENTERTAINMENT

CITY **WHERE TO START?**
You can feel the heartbeat of urban life into the early hours around **Rudolfsplatz** and **Judenplatz** (126 C–D2) *(𝒰 K–L 7–8)*. Other popular districts are the Museums-Quartier and neighbouring Spittelberg, the Naschmarkt area – especially the Freihaus Quarter along Schleifmühlgasse – and in the vicinity of Margaretenplatz. There are many bars and music pubs along the Gürtel between Lerchenfelderstraße, Alserstraße and Florianigasse.

Things are really happening in Vienna these days. Since the city emerged from being overshadowed by the Iron Curtain and found its place in the heart of a united Central Europe, it has had a cultural and nightlife scene that can be compared with those in Paris and London.

Of course, the main attractions are still major institutions, like the State Opera, Musikverein and Konzerthaus, that gave the city its reputation as a metropolis of traditional culture. There is a never-ending stream of the crème de la crème from the world of classical music performing here. The Burgtheater has also been able to preserve its rank as one of the leading

Photo: Loos Bar

Arias and satirical cabaret in *BeisIn*, musicals and techno: Vienna's cultural scene provides something for all tastes every evening

theatres in the German-speaking world under Matthias Hartmann, who has been its director since 2009.

Apart from these venues, the city also offers a wealth of other events which are listed in the weekly 'what's on' magazine *Falter* and many of the dailies. From light comedy to biting satire, from arias to heavy-metal gigs, and hit musicals to experimental theatre, Vienna has evening entertainment to satisfy all tastes. Many top venues, however, are closed during the main tourist season in July and August – including, the four main national theatres. This is compensated for by series of events such as the 'Klangbogen' or the music film festival in front of the Town Hall, and the countless theatre and operetta festivals, concerts and readings held in and around Austria's capital city.

Swinging saxes: lovers of traditional jazz will feel at home in Jazzland

BARS & MUSIC PUBS

ARENA (141 E3) (*ℳ P11*)
Time-honoured alternative stage for everything from oldie rock and punk to reggae and techno. *Baumgasse 80 | www.arena.co.at | bus 80A, U3 Erdberg*

INSIDER TIP B 72 (132 A3) (*ℳ G7*)
Music pub without food; occasionally live music from electro to rock. *Daily 8pm–4am | Stadtbahnbogen 72 | www.b72.at | U6 Alser Straße*

BLUE BOX (138 B1) (*ℳ H10*)
Club music, seventies, ska and more. Different DJ programme every day. Good international and vegetarian cooking, breakfast until the afternoon. *Mon–Thu 10am–2am, Fri and Sat 10am–4am | Richtergasse 8 | www.bluebox.at | bus 13A, U3 Neubaugasse*

THE BOX
(127 F4) (*ℳ M 8–9*)
Exclusive, sophisticated and very chic. The Box in the cellar of the Hilton Hotel is the place for night owls to party with cosmopolitan flair and the finest sound imaginable. *Thu–Sat and the night before holidays from 10pm | Am Stadtpark 3 | entrance Landstraßer Hauptstraße 2 | www.thebox-vienna.at | U4 Landstraße/Wien Mitte*

CAFE CONCERTO
(132 A4) (*ℳ G8*)
The place to have fun in and a somewhat-different cosy Viennese café: live music from jazz and folk to Oriental world music and readings are offered on the three floors. With a chill-out zone, winter garden and party cellar. *Tue–Sat from 7pm, cellar from 9pm | Lerchenfelder Gürtel 53 | www.cafeconcerto.at | U6 Thaliastraße*

INSIDER TIP ▶ CHELSEA
(132 A5) (𝄢 G 8)

Rock, house, Brit and Indie pop – full, loud, great DJs. *Mon–Sat 6pm–4am | Lerchenfelder Gürtel/ U-Bahn-Bögen 29–30 | www.chelsea.co.at | U6 Thaliastraße*

DONAU (132 C6) (𝄢 J 9)

Extremely hip and with one of the longest bars in town. *Mon–Thu 8pm–2am, Fri, Sat 8pm–6am, Sun 8pm–4am | Karl-Schweighofer-Gasse 10 | www.donautechno.com | tram 49, bus 2 A, U2 Museumsquartier*

FLEX ★
(133 E3) (𝄢 K6)

Underground, live, in a bunker next to the underground for die-hard lovers of pandemonium – from drum 'n' bass, noise and jungle to hardcore. *Daily 8pm–4am | Donaukanalpromenade/Augartenbrücke | www.flex.at | U2, U4 Schottenring*

HALBESTADT
(128 C6) (𝄢 H5)

American bar without excessive chic; wonderful long drinks. *Mon–Thu 7pm–2am, Fri and Sat 7pm–4am | Stadtbahnbogen 155, opposite Währinger Gürtel 146 | www.halbestadt.at | U6 Nussdorfer Straße*

JAZZLAND (127 D1) (𝄢 L8)

Dixieland, blues, boogie, swing: Jazzland is the top address for lovers of traditional jazz. *Mon–Sat 7pm–2am | Franz-Josefs-Kai 29 | www.jazzland.at | tram 1, 2, U1, U4 Schwedenplatz*

LOOS BAR
(127 D4) (𝄢 K8)

American bar and a place of pilgrimage for the aesthetically minded – designed by the master Adolf Loos himself. *Sun–Wed noon–4am, Thu–Sat noon–5am | Kärntner Durchgang 10 | www.loosbar.at | U1, U3 Stephansplatz*

INSIDER TIP ▶ PLANTER'S CLUB
(126 C1) (𝄢 K 7)

The extravagantly decorated bar with the flair of colonial days has a gigantic selection of drinks. You can fortify yourself next door in *Livingstone* with exotic Californian specialities before you start imbibing! *Club Sun–Wed 5pm–2am, Thu–Sat 5pm–4am, Livingstone daily 5pm–1.30am | Zelinkagasse 4 | www.plantersclub.com | tram 1, U2, U4 Schottenring*

★ Flex
For fans of underground music: high-decibel 'in' spot in a bunker next to the underground
→ p. 83

★ Passage
Top DJs and cool surroundings in one of the city's top dance temples → p. 84

★ Musikverein
The world's best acoustics: the highest level of performances of classical music → p. 87

★ Theater an der Wien
Superb opera, intimate atmosphere → p. 88

★ Burgtheater
Theatrical icons in the flagship of thespian art in German → p. 89

★ Staatsoper
The embodiment of Austrian musical culture → p. 87

★ Theater in der Josefstadt
Theatrical art for the bourgeoisie → p. 89

MARCO POLO HIGHLIGHTS

CLUBS & DISCOS

PORGY & BESS (127 E4) (*m L8*)
Ambitious programme for jazz fans –
live gigs almost every night. *Daily from
7.30pm | Riemergasse 11 | www.porgy.at |
U3 Stubentor*

SZENE WIEN (141 D6) (*m O*)
Concerts from experimental to rock music –
usually in the 'hard' department: punk,
rock, techno or rave. *Hauffgasse 26 | www.
szenewien.com | tram 71 Hauffgasse*

CLUBS & DISCOS

Some discos organise regular clubbings
and raves. Dates in the 'Falter' weekly
magazine and from *Jugend-Info | tel. 17 99.*

INSIDER TIP ▶ FLORIDITA
(127 D4) (*m L9*)
This Cuban dance bar is the hot spot of
Vienna's Latino scene. Salsa courses every
evening to prepare you for the hot rhythms.
*Daily from 7pm | Johannesgasse 3 | www.
floridita.at | U1, U4 Karlsplatz/Oper*

LADERAUM (127 F2) (*m L–M 8*)
The belly of this bathing ship anchored
permanently in the Danube Canal with a
swimming pool on the deck, turns into
one of the most popular clubs in town in
the evening. The DJs play everything from
disco to minimal; there is a dance floor,
a mini-stage for live acts and an excellent
range of drinks at the bar. *All year Wed–
Sat from 11pm | Schwedenplatz | www.
badeschiff.at | U4 Schwedenplatz*

OST KLUB (139 E2) (*m L10*)
Unusual – and only occasionally main-
stream – sounds from Central and (South)
Eastern Europe ring out in this club. You
can stock up on calories in the pleasant
Ost Bar on the same premises. *Daily from
7pm | Schwarzenbergplatz 10 | www.ost-
klub.at | U1, U2, U4 Karlsplatz*

PASSAGE ★ (126 B5) (*m K9*)
One of the top dance palaces. Here, under
the Burgring in the cool atmosphere of the
Babenberger Passage, top DJs play house,

Mega-cool dance temple: coloured neon lights shine on guests in black-and-white in Passage

dance floor, r 'n' b and much more. *Tue–Sat from 8pm or 10pm | www.sunshine.at | tram 1 Babenbergerstraße, U2 Museumsquartier*

SASS (127 D6) (*[]* K9)

Ultra-chic, in-place with large dance floor, extremely varied music programme, fabulous sound equipment and just-as-fabulous bar. *Wed–Sun from 10pm | Karlsplatz 1 | www.sassvienna.com | U1, U2, U4 Karlsplatz*

VOLKSGARTEN DISCO AND PAVILION (126 B4) (*[]* J8)

Good address for the 25-to-35-year-old crowd. Music: a great deal of latest experimental sounds. Atmosphere: plush, mirrors, plants, kidney-shaped tables. In summer, INSIDERTIP▸ ballroom dancing from 6pm–11pm in the Volksgarten's Tanzcafé. *April–Sept daily 11am–2am, Clubbing Thu–Sat 11pm–6am | Burggarten 1 | www.volksgarten.at | tram D, 1, 46, 49, U2, U3 Volkstheater*

EINFAHRT (133 F3) (*[]* L7)

Einfahrt not only provides its guests with drinks, snacks and all kinds of newspapers but also stimulating events on more than 200 evenings a year – live jazz, readings, cabaret, discussions. *Mon–Fri 11am–1am, Sat 10am–5pm | Haidgasse 3/Karmelitermarkt | tel. 9 42 68 86 | www.einfahrt.at | tram 2, 21, U2 Taborstraße*

KULISSE (142 C3) (*[]* E7)

The pioneer theatre for all kinds of cabaret with a message is located in an old suburban pub – food and drinks are served during performances. *Rosensteingasse 39 | tel. 4 85 38 70 | www.kulisse.at | tram 9, 44 Mayssengasse*

METROPOL (142 C3) (*[]* F7)

Equally as laid-back Viennese as the *Kulisse* but with more emphasis placed on concerts and musicals. The Metropol also has a small hall 'Metropoldi' and an open-air stage in the garden. *Hernalser Hauptstraße 55 | tel. 4 07 77 40 | www.wiener-metropol.at | tram 43 Rosensteingasse*

NIEDERMAIR (126 A3) (*[]* J8)

Meritorious small theatre where many satirists celebrated their first successes and where stars also like to appear. *Lenaugasse 1 A | tel. 4 08 44 92 | www.niedermair.at | tram 2 U2 Rathaus*

INSIDERTIP▸ ORIGINAL WIENER STEGREIFBÜHNE (142 C3) (*[]* C8)

Light comedies – off the cuff: no matter how ridiculous the basic plot, the jokes and spontaneity of the actors, as well as the down-to-earth reaction of the audience, always a great evening out. *Only mid-June–Sept | Maroltingergasse 43 | tel. 9 14 54 14 | www.tschauner.at | bus 48 A, tram 10, 46 Joachimsthalerplatz*

CINEMAS

CINEMAS

INSIDER TIP ▶ STADTSAAL
(138 B2) (*Ø H10*)

Cabaret theatre seating 360. This is where stars and promising talents appear; also international guest performers. Performances (almost) every evening. *Mariahilfer Straße 8 | tel. 9 09 22 44 | www.stadtsaal.com | U3 Neubaugasse*

WUK (132 B2) (*Ø H6*)

Autonomous studio and culture house with music and dance performances, concerts, readings and exhibitions. *Währinger Straße 59 | tel. 4 01 21 10 | www.wuk.at | tram 5, 33, 37, 38, 40–42, U6 Volksoper*

CINEMAS

INSIDER TIP ▶ BELLARIA
(126 A4) (*Ø J9*)

Austrian nostalgia from the years before and shortly after the war and art films in the original version in the evening. *Museumstraße 3 | tel. 5 23 75 91 | bus 48 A, U2 Volkstheater*

FILMMUSEUM (126 C4) (*Ø K9*)

A cineaste's mecca: celluloid rarities from around the world are screened every evening. *Summer break July/Aug | Augustinerstraße 1 | tel. 5 33 70 54 | www.filmmuseum.at | tram D, 1, 2, U1, U2, U4 Karlsplatz*

OPEN-AIR CINEMAS

You can see many interesting films – some in the original language – in charming open-air cinemas during the warm summer months (incl. *www.arena.co.at | www.kinountersternen.at | www.schlosskino.at | www.kinowienochnie.at | www.volxkino.at*).

CONCERTS

KONZERTHAUS (127 E6) (*Ø L9*)

The dazzlingly white Jugendstil building is a stronghold of modern classics – Mahler, Bartók, Stravinsky – as well as contemporary music. There are also regular performances of all other musical styles from Baroque to Renaissance, from pop to jazz,

Nostalgic foyer of the Bellaria Cinema: Tear-jerkers from the good old days in the afternoon

in the various halls. The Vienna Symphony is this institution's in-house orchestra that has always considered itself more progressive than the conservative Musikverein. *Lothringer Straße 20 | tel. 24 20 02 | www. konzerthaus.at | tram D, 71, U4 Stadtpark*

KURSALON (127 E5) (*M L9*)

Good solid performances of melodies in ¾ time by Lanner, Strauss & Co. are given in this pleasure pavilion on the edge of the Stadtpark. Towards the end of the concerts, the audience is encouraged to get up and trip the light fantastic – something that is unusual in the capital city of the waltz, by the way. *Johannesgasse 33 | ticket tel. 5 12 57 90 | www.kursalonwien. at | tram 2, U4 Stadtpark*

MUSIKVEREIN ★ ● (127 D6) (*M L9*)

The 'Gesellschaft der Musikfreunde' (Society of the Friends of Music) commissioned the Ringstraße architect Theophil von Hansen with this building, which was erected between 1867 and 1869. Its main concert hall, the 'Golden Hall', has probably the finest acoustics in the world and has hosted all the major stars ranging from Bruckner, Mahler and Strauss to Karajan in the last 140 years or so. It has remained a bastion of classical traditions to this day. As the home of the Vienna Philharmonic Orchestra it regularly welcomes the most famous international orchestras, conductors and soloists. Four small ultra-modern halls in the cellar. *Bösendorferstraße 12 | tel. 5 05 81 90 | www.musikverein.at | tram D, 1, 2, 62, 65, U1, U2, U4 Karlsplatz*

RADIO KULTURHAUS (139 E2) (*M L10*)

The innovative culture centre in the house of the Austrian national radio organisation. There are concerts of all kinds of music, readings, discussions, etc. in the main studio on most days. *Argentinerstraße*

30A | tel. 50 10 10 and 50 17 03 77 | radio kulturhaus.orf.at | U1 Taubstummengasse

OPERA, OPERETTA, MUSICALS

L.E.O. (138 A3) (*M M9*)

Mini-versions of Verdi, Puccini and Co. for two soloists plus piano and the audience as the choir in the 'Letzten Erfreulichen Operntheater' (Last Satisfying Opera Theatre) – Viennese cabaret art with tremendous charm! *Ungargasse 18 | tel. 7 12 14 27 | www.theaterleo.at | U4 Landstraße/ Wien Mitte*

RAIMUNDTHEATER (138 A3) (*M G11*)

Operettas were produced here for decades but today musicals such as 'Beauty and the Beast'. 'Grease' and 'Phantom of the Opera' are staged in this theatre. *Wallgasse 18–20 | tel. 59 97 70 | tickets tel. 5 88 85 | www.musicalvienna.at | tram 6, 18, U6 Gumpendorfer Straße*

RONACHER (127 D4–5) (*M L9*)

Beautifully renovated variety theatre in the Belle Epoque style. It has been used for musicals, variety and guest musical performances since reopening a few years ago. *Seilerstätte 9 | tel. 51 41 10 | tickets tel. 5 88 85 | www.musicalvienna.at | U1, U3 Stephansplatz*

STAATSOPER ★ ● (126 C5) (*M K9*)

The State Opera – the 'House on the Ringstraße' – symbolises Vienna's position as a music metropolis in way that can only be compared with that of the Musikverein. Since its opening in 1869, almost all the world's greatest opera singers have appeared on its stage and the most famous conductors have led the orchestra. Performances of more than 40 different operas are given during the 10 months of the season– from 1 September to 30 June.

The Vienna Philharmonic is the State Opera's orchestra.

Ticket prices range from 8 euros (seats with a limited view of the stage) to 240 euros. Standing room tickets cost 3 euros but you will have to queue up for hours before sought-after performances to get one. It is a advisable to book tickets in advance from the Bundestheaterverband (Federal Theatre Association). You can possibly buy tickets shortly before performances from ticket agencies and the porters at good hotels often know how to make the impossible possible – however, there is always an extra charge for these services. The tent erected on the rooftop terrace which is used for INSIDER TIP opera for children is extremely successful! *Opernring 2 | tel. 51 44 40 | www.staatsoper.at | tram D, 1, 2, 62, 65, bus 59A, U1, U2, U4 Karlsplatz*

THEATER AN DER WIEN ★
(126 B6) (*ɯ K9*)

The first performance of the first version of Beethoven's 'Fidelio' was given in this theatre that opened its doors in 1801. Many other plays by Kleist, Grillparzer, Raimund and Nestroy as well as operettas by Strauss, Suppé, Millöcker, Zeller, Lehár, Kálmán and others were premiered here. From 1945–55, it acted as the temporary home of the State Opera and was then used for musicals and guest performances during the Vienna Festival Weeks in May and June. The Theater an der Wien now operates once again as a year-round opera house. *Linke Wienzeile 6 | tel. 5 88 85 | www.theater-wien.at | U4 Kettenbrückengasse, U1, U2, U4 Karlsplatz*

VOLKSOPER (132 B1) (*ɯ H5*)

The 'little' sister of the State Opera specialises in light – and some not so light – operas, operettas and the occasional musical; the performances often have a very high standard. *Währinger Straße 78 | tel. 51 44 40 | www.volksoper.at | tram 40 to 42, U6 Währinger Straße/Volksoper*

INSIDER TIP WIENER KAMMEROPER
(127 E3) (*ɯ L8*)

The Wiener Kammeroper, which used to be famous for its unconventional productions with still-unknown singers, has now been taken over by the Theater an der Wien. Its intention is to create an ensemble of young singers and perform small-scale operas. The first season 2011/12 lists five different productions. *Fleischmarkt 24 | tel. 5 88 85 | www.theater-wien.at | bus 2A, U4 Schwedenplatz*

LOW BUDGET

▶ A kind of open-air urban living room has developed in the spacious inner courtyard area of the *MuseumsQuartier* (126 A–B 4–5) (*ɯ J9*) cultural district. It is very popular and open until late at night. There are bars, seating to lounge around in, model car races, chess tables, a gigantic sandpit for boccia (no charge!), free readings and concerts, DJs, children's festivals and artistic events throughout the summer. In winter, igloos, mulled-wine sellers and a skating rink attract lots of visitors. *Museumsplatz 1 | tram 49, bus 2A, 48A, U2, U3 Volkstheater or Museumsquartier | www.mqw.at/sommer and www.mqw.at/winter respectively*

▶ The *Volxkino,* an open-air touring cinema sets up its large screen at various places in the districts outside of the city centre and shows cinematic treats free of charge. *Tel. 2 19 85 45 80 | www.volxkino.at*

The peak of theatrical art: tickets for the Burgtheater are very much in demand

THEATRE

AKADEMIETHEATER (127 E6) (*∭ L9*)
This offshoot of the Burgtheater shares the same ensemble as the big brother and presents mainly 20th-century classics and contemporary drama. *Lisztstraße 1 | tel. 51 44 40 | www.burgtheater.at | tram D, 71, U4 Stadtpark*

BURGTHEATER ★ ● (126 B3) (*∭ J8*)
The flagship of thespian art in German. During the Claus Peymann era (1989–99), there was great deal of controversy between the director, some performers in the ensemble and the press, as well as the more conservative members of the audience. Under the leadership of Matthias Hartmann, it still guarantees performances of classical and modern plays of the highest standard. There is also a very good bookshop in the foyer. *Dr.-Karl-Lueger-Ring 2 | tel. 51 44 40 | www.burgtheater.at | tram D, 1, U3 Herrengasse*

THEATER IN DER JOSEFSTADT ★
(132 B4) (*∭ H8*)
This stronghold of sound plays and light comedy, with occasional forays into classic and modern drama, is becoming increasingly daring with more innovative works and productions. *Josefstädter Str. 26 | tel. 42 70 03 00 | www.josefstadt.org | tram 2 Theater in der Josefstadt*

VIENNA'S ENGLISH THEATRE
(132 C4) (*∭ H8*)
This small, but excellent, theatre presents first-rate light comedies and some classical plays. *Josefsgasse 12 | tel. 40 21 26 00 | www.englishtheatre.at | U2 Lerchenfelder Straße*

VOLKSTHEATER
(132 C5) (*∭ J9*)
Traditional theatre with a broad repertoire, large ensemble and socio-critical attitude. *Neustiftgasse 1 | tel. 52 11 10 | www.volks theater.at | U2, U3 Volkstheater*

WHERE TO STAY

With more than 10 million overnight stays every year, Vienna is one of the top tourist destinations in Europe. Regardless of whether it is an elegant palais on the Ringstraße from the late 19th century, a simple youth hostel or a grain silo on the Danube that has been turned into a luxury hotel: there is a fantastic selection for all tastes and budgets.

On average, a pleasantly comfortable double room close to the centre will cost 100–150 euros. You can find cheaper rooms, but you will have to reduce your expectations. It is hard to find anything under 50 euros unless you are prepared to stay in a hostel.

In Vienna, as in the rest of Austria, hotels are divided into five categories – from the five stars of the luxury class to simple hotels with only one. The guesthouses in the centre are something particularly Viennese. They are usually small places in residential or office buildings that concentrate on bed and breakfast; they are often personally run by the owner and have their own individual character.

The so-called 'season hotels' offer reasonably priced accommodation in student halls of residence that are run as hotels during the summer holidays from 1 July to 30 September (bookings: *Österreichische Hochschülerschaft | tel. 31 08 88 00*).

Photo: Suite in the Hotel Imperial

No matter where you want to stay – on the slopes of the Vienna Woods or in the city centre – we let you know the best places

Another alternative – even for short stays – is to hire a flat. The Viennese Tourist Association can provide you with a free list of accommodation in Vienna. However, the prices are not always 100% accurate. This also applies to those quoted by Wien Tourismus under *www. wien.info.at* which can also make telephone reservations for you *(daily 9am–7pm | tel. 2 45 55)*.

HOTELS: EXPENSIVE

CORDIAL THEATER HOTEL WIEN ★
(132 B–C4) *(Ø H8)*
This plush, centrally-located 4-star hotel has a slightly old-fashioned atmosphere. Not cheap, but pleasant. Excellent breakfast buffet. *54 rooms | Josefstädter Straße 22 | tel. 4 05 36 48 | www.cordial.at | tram 2, bus 13A Lederergasse*

Das Triest: rooms designer with a love of detail

10 | tel. 51 58 40 | www.kvu.at | bus 2A, U1, U3 Stephansplatz

THE LEVANTE PARLIAMENT
(126 A3) (*ш J8*)

This boutique hotel charms its guests with its modern interior design created using a great deal of choice wood, natural stone and unique glass objects. The hi-tech equipment is just as first-rate as the 24-hour service. Another plus point: undisturbed sleep; most of the rooms open onto the quiet inner courtyard where you can also relax in the more than 4000ft² garden during the day. 70 rooms | Auerspergstraße 9 | tel. 22 82 80 | www.thelevante.com | U2 Rathaus

OPERNRING (126 C5) (*ш K9*)

This building with 35 large rooms exudes real old-Viennese charm. You live in a perfect location diagonally across from the State Opera. Opernring 11 | tel. 5 87 55 18 | www.opernring.at | tram D, 1, 2, bus 57 A, U1, U2, U4 Karlsplatz

RADISSON BLU STYLE HOTEL ★
(126 C3) (*ш K8*)

Italianità rubs shoulders with Viennese tradition in this extremely chic designer hotel. Each room is individually decorated with alabaster, precious wood, satin and silk, hi-tech equipment from flat-screen TV to wireless broadband internet, quality service and comfort. Other highlights: the wine bar and Italian gourmet restaurant. 78 rooms | Herrengasse 12 | tel. 22 78 00 | www.radissonblu.com | U3 Herrengasse

GRAND HOTEL BIEDERMEIER WIEN ★
(134 B5) (*ш M9*)

This comfortable, stylish 4-star hotel is perfect if you want to enjoy the charm of early 19th-century Vienna. The complex includes an arcade with a great deal of atmosphere – the only one from the Biedermeier period in Europe to have been preserved in its original state. Landstraßer Hauptstraße 28 | tel. 71 67 10 | www.mercure.com | bus 74, U3 Rochusgasse

KÖNIG VON UNGARN (127 E3) (*ш L8*)

A hotel like a private city palais and only a 1-minute walk from St Stephen's. The furnishing is unassuming and well cared for. Lovely foyer with bar in the glass-roofed inner courtyard. 33 rooms | Schulerstraße

RATHAUS WEIN & DESIGN ★
(132 C4) (*ш H8*)

This 4-star hotel is the delight of all wine-lovers. Each of the 33 rooms has a top wine-grower as its patron and a special fridge with their best vintages waiting to be tasted. In addition, there is a wine lounge and wine shop, perfect service, comfort and chic design, not to forget the convenient location near the centre in the old-Viennese Josefstadt district. *Lange Gasse 13 | tel. 4 00 11 22 | www.hotel-rathaus-wien.at | tram 2, bus 13A Lederer-gasse/Josefstädter Straße, U3 Lerchen-felder Straße*

REGINA (126 B1) (*Ⓜ J7*)

Renowned, high-quality hotel with ele-gantly decorated rooms in a city palais. Near the Ringstraße. *164 rooms | Roose-veltplatz 15 | tel. 40 44 60 | www.krems lehnerhotels.at | tram 37, 38, 40–44, U2 Schottentor*

INSIDER TIP DAS TRIEST
(139 D2) (*Ⓜ K10*)

London's star designer Terence Conran paid great attention to detail when he created this gem of a modern 5-star hotel in the former stables of the imperial stagecoach company. *73 rooms | Wiedner Hauptstraße 12 | tel. 58 91 80 | www.dastriest.at | tram 62, 65, U1, U2, U4 Karlsplatz*

HOTEL WANDL ⭐ (127 D3) (*Ⓜ K8*)

This traditional, elegant hotel in an ex-ceptionally central location has been in the ownership of the same family since 1854: the Graben and St Stephen's are just a few steps away. The hotel does not have a car park and drivers should use one of the multi-stories. *138 rooms | Peters-platz 9 | tel. 53 45 50 | www.hotel-wandl. com | bus 2A, U1, U3 Stephansplatz*

HOTELS: MODERATE

HOTEL AM AUGARTEN
(134 B2) (*Ⓜ M6*)

In the immediate vicinity of two green oases, the Augarten and Prater. Cheerful, bright and spotless. *65 rooms | Heine-straße 15 | tel. 2 14 35 07 | www.austria-hotels.at | U2 Taborstraße*

CAPRI (134 A3) (*Ⓜ M7*)

Smart, personally run hotel, in a function-ally modern style. Each room has a sitting area, most have a balcony – some facing the sunny inner courtyard. *70 rooms |*

⭐ **Cordial Theater Hotel Wien**
Plush, comfortable 4-star hotel → **p. 91**

⭐ **Grand Hotel Biedermeier Wien**
Live like Franz Schubert, but with considerably more comfort → **p. 92**

⭐ **Rathaus Wein & Design**
Smart designer hotel for wine lovers → **p. 92**

⭐ **Radisson Blu Style Hotel**
Extremely chic hotel combining tradition and hi-tech → **p. 92**

⭐ **Hotel Wandl**
Elegant and informal, traditional and un-beatably centrally located → **p. 93**

⭐ **Pension Arenberg**
Tasteful but cosy Ring-straße building near the Danube Canal → **p. 95**

⭐ **Stadthalle**
Charming, creatively decorated lodgings for the environmentally conscious → **p. 97**

⭐ **Strandhotel Alte Donau**
Friendly, unpretentious hotel with its own beach → **p. 97**

⭐ **Wombat's**
Well-run hostel on the Naschmarkt near the railway station → **p. 99**

MARCO POLO HIGHLIGHTS

*Praterstraße 44–46 | tel. 2 14 84 04 | www.
hotelcapri.at | U1 Nestroyplatz*

FÜRSTENHOF (132 A6) (*∅ G10*)

A pleasant hotel for families, conveniently located opposite the Westbahnhof.
10% reduction for e-mail reservations. *58
rooms | Neubaugürtel 4 | tel. 5 23 32 67 |
www.hotel-fuerstenhof.com | tram 6, 9, 18,
U3, U6 Westbahnhof*

INSIDER TIP ▶ HOLLMANN BELETAGE
(127 E3) (*∅ L8*)

Surprisingly affordable stylish gem of a
home-away-from-home in the heart of city
centre. Minimalist, Asian-inspired design
with a lot of wood and leather, hip furniture, lobby with a piano, open fireplace and
books. The chef himself, Robert Hollmann,
cooks in the hotel's restaurant. *25 rooms |
Köllnerhofgasse 6 | tel. 9 611960 | www.
hollmann-beletage.at | U1, U4 Schwedenplatz*

KÄRNTNERHOF
(127 E3) (*∅ L8*)

You can stay in a comfortable, old hotel
without any frills but with a cosy atmosphere, in the heart of the historical centre
of Vienna, not even three minutes from

LUXURY HOTELS

Bristol (127 D5) (*∅ K9*)

Fin-de-siècle hotel with lots of marble
and gold, silk and velvet – and well-off
guests from the aristocracy and world
of culture. Fantastic location opposite
the opera house at the beginning of
Kärntner Straße. One of the so-called
'wild young men' is the chef of the hotel
restaurant, the *Korso. 140 rooms |
from 233 euros | Kärntner Ring 1 |
tel. 51 51 60 | www.hotelbristol.at |
tram D, 1, 2, U1, U2, U4 Karlsplatz*

Imperial (129 D5–6) (*∅ L9*)

This is where state guests spend the
night. The paintings on the ceilings in
the rooms, the valuable carpets, the
old paintings, exquisite period furniture
and marble staircase make this more
than 100-year-old former city palais a
magnificent museum where you can
stay the night. *138 rooms | from 323
euros | Kärntner Ring 16 | tel. 50 11 00 |
www.hotelimperialwien.at | tram D, 1, 2,
U1, U2, U4 Karlsplatz*

Sacher (126–127 C–D5) (*∅ K9*)

Like the chocolate cake of the same
name, this hotel – which was opened in
1876 – has been a symbol of Vienna since
the days of the empire. One of the city's
finest private art collections has been
hung in the elegant, but comfortable,
rooms and suites following the total
renovation of the building. *152 rooms |
from 395 euros | Philharmonikerstraße
4 | tel. 5 14 56 | www.sacher.com | tram
D, 1, 2, U1, U2, U4 Karlsplatz*

Sofitel Vienna Stephansdom ☼
(127 E–F2) (*∅ M7*)

The hyper-modern 5-star hotel designed
by star architect Jean Nouvel dazzles its
guests with a spectacular illuminated
façade and futuristic hi-tech atmosphere. The rooms and gourmet rooftop
restaurant have fairy-tale views over
Vienna's city centre. *182 rooms | from
325 euros | Praterstraße 1 | tel. 90 61 60 |
www.sofitel.com | tram 1, 2, U1, U4
Schwedenplatz*

St Stephen's. *43 rooms | Grashofgasse 4 | tel. 5 12 19 23 | www.karntnerhof.com | U1, U3 Stephansplatz*

KUNSTHOF
(134 B2) *(ⓜ M6)*

A comfortable hotel in a late-Classicist building. Young artists regularly redecorate the lobby, library and staircase. The rooms are sensible and modern, bright and colourfully furnished. Breakfast and bar in the green inner courtyard. *49 rooms | Mühlfeldgasse 13 | tel. 2 14 31 78 | www. hotelkunsthof.at | U1, Schnellbahn Wien Nord Praterstern*

PENSION ARENBERG ⭐
(127 F3) *(ⓜ M8)*

This elegant but cosy guesthouse with 22 rooms is conveniently located on the edge of the Old Town not far away from the Danube Canal. *Stubenring 2 | tel. 5 12 52 91 | www.arenberg.at | tram 2, U3 Stubentor*

INSIDER TIP ▶ PENSION NOSSEK
(126 C3) *(ⓜ K8)*

Well cared-for family guesthouse with Viennese charm in the pedestrian precinct two minute's walk from St Stephen's. Payment in cash only! *31 rooms | Graben 17 | tel. 5 33 70 41 | www.pension-nossek.at | bus 1 A, 2 A, 3 A, U1, U3 Stephansplatz*

PENSION SPIESS & SPIESS
(140 B1) *(ⓜ N9)*

First-rate 4-star guesthouse with comparatively moderate prices; elegant, straightforward design, large rooms, half of them with balconies, very personal service. *7 rooms | Hainburgerstraße 19 | tel. 7 14 85 05 | www.spiess-vienna.at | U3 Rochusgasse*

POST (127 E3) *(ⓜ L8)*

The traditional hotel where Mozart, Wagner and Nietzsche once laid their

Viennese charm: Pension Nossek's breakfast room

heads has now been completely renovated into a smart, pleasant 3-star hotel. Very centrally located. *104 rooms | Fleischmarkt 24 | tel. 5 15 8 30 | www.hotel-post-wien.at | U1, U4 Schwedenplatz*

ZUR WIENER STAATSOPER
(127 D5) *(ⓜ L9)*

Standard family hotel with a pleasant atmosphere and most modern comforts. Many of the main sights are just around the corner. *22 rooms | Krugerstraße 11 | tel. 5 13 12 74 | www.zurwienerstaatsoper.at | tram D, 1, 2, U1, U2, U4 Karlsplatz*

HOTELS: BUDGET

AUSTRIA CLASSIC NORDBAHN
(134 B3) *(ⓜ M7)*

Spruce, inexpensive 3-star hotel near the Prater with pleasant service and a sauna.

78 rooms | Praterstraße 72 | tel. 211300 | www.classic-hotelwien.at | U1 Nestroyplatz

INSIDER TIP BENEDIKTUSHAUS
(126 C2) (*ⓜ K8*)

It would be hard to find a hotel with a more central location than here in the time-honoured Schottenstift. And hardly a more peaceful one – thanks to the monastery's courtyard. The contemplative atmosphere is further increased by the private chapel. *21rooms | Freyung 6 A | tel. 53 49 89 00 | www.benediktushaus. at | U2 Schottentor, U3 Herrengasse, U4 Schottenring*

BETA ART (137 D4) (*ⓜ E12*)

The place for price-conscious design fans: no-frills aesthetics in chic contrasting red-and-white, top-notch technical equipment and attentive, personal service. All rooms are decorated with works created by young artists and sculptors. Meeting places: the unconventionally designed breakfast room and hotel bar. *43 rooms | Sechshauser Straße 83 | tel. 8 92 13 87 | beta-art-wien. hotel-rv.com | U4 Schönbrunn, bus 57A Hollergasse*

INSIDER TIP BOLTZMANN ARCOTEL
(132 C2) (*ⓜ J6*)

Small, chic boutique hotel in a district full of houses from the late 19th century, not far from the famous Strudlhofstiege. Personal atmosphere, excellent value for money. *70 rooms | Boltzmanngasse 8 | tel. 31 61 20 | www.arcotel.at | tram 37, 38, 40 to 42 Sensengasse*

GABRIEL (140 C3) (*ⓜ O11*)

Charming, medium-sized hotel in a quiet location. Rooms with TV and telephone. Parking spaces. *55 rooms | Landstraßer Hauptstraße 165 | tel. 7 12 32 05 | www. adler-hotels-wien.at | bus 74A, tram18, U3 Schlachthausgasse*

GEBLERGASSE (132 A3) (*ⓜ G7*)

Peacefully located hotel near the Gürtel and underground; recently-renovated rooms, pleasant lounge with bar and free Internet terminals, buffet breakfast for 5 euros per person. *96 rooms | Geblergasse 21 | tel. 4 06 33 66 | www.geblergasse.com | U6 Alser Straße, tram 44*

KAFFEEMÜHLE
(132 A6) (*ⓜ G9*)

Pleasant guesthouse near the Mariahilfer Straße shopping street. The 24 rooms all have cable TV. Parking space. *Kaiserstraße 45 | tel. 5 23 86 88 | www.kaffeemuehle. at | U6 Burggasse*

KUGEL (138 B1) (*ⓜ H9*)

This economical and beautifully renovated hotel is located near the picturesque Biedermeier Spittelberg district. *34 rooms | Siebensterngasse 43 | tel. 5 23 33 55 | www.hotelkugel.at | tram 49, bus 2A, 13A Siebensterngasse*

PENSION CITY (127 D3) (*ⓜ L8*)

This peaceful B&B with 19 stylish rooms is located on the 2nd floor of the house the Austrian writer Franz Grillparzer was born in and only two minute's walk from St Stephen's. *Bauernmarkt 10 | tel. 5 33 95 21 | www.citypension.at | bus 2A, 3A, U1, U3 Stephansplatz*

PENSION NEUER MARKT
(127 D4) (*ⓜ K8*)

Modern, comfortable guesthouse perfectly located halfway between the State Opera and St Stephen's. *37 rooms | Seilergasse 9 | tel. 5 12 23 16 | www.hotelpension. at | bus 3 A, U1, U3 Stephansplatz*

ROOMZ (141 F4) (*ⓜ Q12*)

Functional simplicity and cool brown, blue, pink and green shades: this budget designer hotel, with its youthful chic, is

Ecologically-focussed Hotel Stadthalle: rooms with a view of the green inner courtyard

comfortably furnished and run with enthusiasm. It is located near the Prater and is easy to reach both from the centre and the airport. Restaurant with an adjacent 24-hour bar in the house, as well as a fitness rooms (open daily 6am–10pm). *152 rooms | Paragonstraße 1 | tel. 7 43 17 77 | www.roomz-vienna.com | U3 Gasometer*

SHERMIN (139 D–E2) (*M K10*)
Pleasant, family-style hotel in a peaceful, very central location almost within sight of Karlskirche. *11 rooms | Rilkeplatz 7 | tel. 58 66 18 30 | www.hotel-pension-shermin. at | U4 Karlsplatz*

STADTHALLE ★ ☺
(137 E1) (*M F10*)
Informal hotel with an unusual atmosphere. Most of the rooms face the green inner courtyard and some have been decorated by artists. Ecology also plays a role with solar power and recycled water. Ideal for cyclists: own bicycle garage and repair shop. *46 rooms | Hackengasse 20 | tel. 9 82 42 72 | www.hotelstadthalle.at | tram 9, 49 Hackengasse, U6 Burggasse/ Stadthalle*

STRANDHOTEL ALTE DONAU ★
(143 E2) (*M R3*)
This friendly, family hotel on the border of the Alte Donau recreation area is only a few minutes from the city centre by underground. Private beach with lawns for sunbathing. *33 rooms | Wagramer Straße 51 | tel. 2 04 40 40 | www.alte-donau.at | U1 Alte Donau*

URANIA (134 B4) (*M M7*)
Novel, well-run 2-star hotel. Each room is individually decorated from medieval to Moorish, Japanese to country style or Baroque. *32 rooms | Obere Weissgerberstraße 7 | tel. 7 13 17 11 | www.hotel-urania. at | tram O Radetzkyplatz*

APARTMENTS

ZIPSER (132 B–C4) (*M H7*)
Charming family-run enterprise behind the Town Hall; bright and cosy. Organic breakfast! Garage. *47 rooms | Lange Gasse 49 | tel. 40 45 40 | www.zipser.at | tram 43, 44 Spitalgasse, 2 Strozzigasse*

APARTMENTS

FLEGER (142 C3) (*M D7*)
The 10 comfortable, 4-star units are 400–600ft² in size and located in the heart of the typical Viennese working-class district of Ottakring. From 74 euros for two people; discounts for longer stays. *Seitenberggasse 19 | tel. 4 86 51 62 | www.fleger.at | tram 2 Johann-Krawarik-Gasse, 44 Römergasse*

LOW BUDGET

▶ The *Odyssee* (132 B6) (*M G9*) shared-accommodation organisation can organise private, reasonably-priced places to stay. Pleasant double rooms from 52 euros; also for short periods. Requests online, by telephone or directly in the office. *Mon–Fri 10am–2pm and 3pm–6pm | Westbahnstraße 19 | tel. 4 02 60 61 | www.odyssee-mwz.at | tram 5 Kaiserstraße/Westbahnstraße, U3 Zieglergasse*

▶ Young people who need a cheap place to lay their head have a good chance of finding what they are looking for at the *Studenten Wohnenbörse*. *Mon–Thu 9am–5pm, Fri 9am–noon | tel. 5 45 24 25 | www.wohnenboerse.at*

▶ Online platforms for private shared-accommodation and inexpensive flats and hotels can be found under: *www.mitwohnzentrale.org/Oesterreich, www.wg-gesucht.de, www.urlaub-urlaub.at, www.urlaub-anbieter.com, www.wienprivat.com* (private Viennese landlords' homepage).

SACHER
(127 D3) (*M L8*)
It can't get any more central than this, nor can it be more economical anywhere near here. Cheerful, comfortable 1 and 2-roomed flats on the 7th floor of a relatively new building directly opposite St Stephen's. From 82 euros a day for two people, extra bed: 20 euros. *Rotenturmstraße 1 | tel. 5 33 32 38 | www.sacher-apartments.at | U1, U3 Stephansplatz*

HOSTELS, SEASON HOTELS & YOUTH HOSTELS

Stays in youth hostels are limited to three nights. If you do not have a youth hostel card, there is an additional charge of 3.50 euros per day.

ALL YOU NEED
Two modern, nicely designed, 3-star lodgings open from 1 July to 30 September. Comfortably equipped, generous buffet breakfast, bicycle garage and tools. From 29 euros per person in a double room. *122 rooms | Grosse Schiffgasse 12* (133 F3) (*M L 7*) *| U2, U4 Schottenring;* and *99 rooms | Schäffergasse 2* (139 D2) (*M K 10*) *| U4 Kettenbrückengasse | both tel. 5 12 74 93 | www.allyouneedhotels.at*

DO STEP INN (137 E2) (*M F10*)
This very pleasant, recently opened place near the completely renovated Westbahnhof offers 30 comfortable hostel rooms (with shared shower/WC) and hotel rooms at unbeatable prices (double rooms from 44 euros). Many extras: peaceful inner courtyard, use of kitchen, laundry service,

Wombat's: enthusiastically well-run, modern hostel with many extras

bicycle rental, sauna, free Internet in the lobby. *Felberstraße 20 | tel. 9 82 33 14 | www.dostepinn.at | U3, U6 Westbahnhof*

JUGENDGÄSTEHAUS HÜTTELDORF-HACKING (142 C3) (*∅ O*)

Youth guesthouse in the green valley of the Wien River near the Lainzer animal sanctuary. Open all year. 307 beds in 1-to-8-bed rooms. From 13 euros including breakfast. *Schlossberggasse 8 | tel. 8 77 15 01 | www.hostel.at | bus 53 B, U4 Hütteldorf*

JUGENDHERBERGE WIEN-MYRTHENGASSE (132 B5) (*∅ H9*)

Cheerful, modern, absolutely ship-shape youth hostel. Open all year. 280 beds in 2-to-6-bed rooms, 16.50 euros including breakfast. *Myrthengasse 7/Neustiftgasse 85 | tel. 52 36 31 60 | www.oejhv.or.at | bus 48A Neubaugasse/Neustiftgasse*

MEININGER (139 E5) (*∅ O*)

Friendly, bright rooms for 1, 2 or more people; dormitories – some mixed, others only for women – all with shower, WC, telephone and TV. Internet terminals and parking spaces at low rates. Dormitory from 12 euros, multi-bed rooms from 18 euros, doubles from 25 euros per person. *68 rooms | Columbusgasse 16 | tel. 7 20 88 14 53 | www.meininger-hotels.com | U1 Keplerplatz*

PORZELLANEUM (133 D2) (*∅ J6*)

Every summer, from the beginning of July to the end of August, this student hall of residence is turned into a pleasant place for tourists to spend the night. TV and recreation room, green inner courtyard, washing machine, low-priced Internet. Single, double and multi-bed rooms for 30, 56 and 100 euros respectively. *51 rooms | Porzellangasse 30 | tel. 3 17 72 82 | www.porzellaneum.sth.ac.at | tram D Seegasse*

WOMBAT'S ★
(137 E2) (*∅ F10*)

This well-run, extremely clean hostel is located near the Westbahnhof and is open 24 hours a day. Bar with terraces, billiard table, laundrette, etc. 260 beds in rooms for 2 to 6 people with shower, WC, safe-deposit box. 10 to 29 euros per person, breakfast 3.50 euros. Branches on Maria-hilfer Straße and the Naschmarkt. *Grangasse 6 | tel. 8 97 23 36 | www.wombats.at | tram 52, 58 Kranzgasse, U3, U6 Westbahnhof*

WALKING TOURS

The tours are marked in green in the street atlas, the pull-out map and on the back cover

BACK TO THE MIDDLE AGES: THROUGH THE HEART OF VIENNA

Your stroll will take you from St Stephen's Cathedral through picturesque, winding streets and secluded courtyards, past the oldest churches and Roman foundations to the former Jewish quarter and, from there, to Hofburg on Heldenplatz. If you want to go inside the sights and maybe even have a break for coffee, you should allow at least half a day for this tour.

You start at the religious centre, and almost certainly the best-known symbol, of Vienna – **Stephansdom** → p. 45. After you have paid the exterior and interior of this filigree sandstone cathedral the respect they are due, walk a few yards from its southwestern corner to Singerstraße. Here, art lovers should pay a visit to the **Schatzkammer des Deutschen Ordens** (Treasury of the Teutonic Knights) *(Tue, Thu, Sat 10am–noon, Wed, Fri 3pm–5pm | entrance fee 4 euros)* at No. 7 to admire the utensils used to celebrate mass, ceremonial vessels and weapons.

As soon as you reach the next corner, turn left onto **Blutgasse** – a model of urban redevelopment with cobblestones, ancient buildings and dreamy inner courtyards. **Mozarthaus** → p. 40 awaits you at the

The emperor, churches, coffeehouses: through the former Jewish quarter, to classic Viennese cafés and up the nearby hills

end of the street. The route now takes you through narrow lanes via Schülerstraße and the Wollzeile to **Bäckerstraße** which is always lively, lined with renowned, fashionable watering holes such as *Café Alt Wien* and the celebrity restaurant *Oswald & Kalb*. To the east, you reach one of the most beautiful squares in Vienna, **Dr.-Ignaz-Seipel-Platz** that is **INSIDER TIP** spectacularly illuminated every evening.

The early-Baroque double-towered façade on the northern side belongs to the **Jesuitenkirche** → p. 36. Austria's **Akademie der Wissenschaften** (Academy of Sciences) has its headquarters in the aula of the Old University on the left. A few yards down Sonnenfelsgasse, turn right, and you will find yourself on the amazingly crooked **Schönlaterngasse**. At No. 7, a strange creature made of stone brings

tecture that is all too often overlooked, before walking past two splendid Baroque buildings – the former Imperial Bohemian Chancellery and Old Town Hall and across Judenplatz with the new Holocaust Memorial and through Drahtgasse to the so-called Hof → p. 32, a surprisingly spacious square full of history.

Cross Naglergasse and Wallnerstraße and make your way to Michaelerplatz. Some years ago, archaeologists excavated the remains of a Roman house in the centre of the square. On the north side, you will see one of the milestones of modern architecture: Looshaus, with its unornamented façade was the subject of much criticism when it was built shortly before the start of World War I. A few years ago, an Austrian bank had this symbol of an entire epoch restored to its original appearance. Since then, the simple elegance of the marble façade and wooden-panelled foyer delight visitors more than ever before.

The Looshaus: no-frills elegance with a marble façade

back memories of the famous saga of the reptile-like basilisk that lived in a well in the courtyard in the 13th century and is said to have scared the wits out of people at the time. Next door, a passage leads into the Heiligenkreuzer Hof → p. 34. Leave it through the gate on the other side, turn right and right again and follow the Fleischmarkt westwards until you reach Rotenturmstraße. The so-called 'Bermuda Triangle', a dynamic bar and *Beisl* district, is just across the street. One of the oldest churches in the city, the Romanesque Ruprechtskirche → p. 43, stands like a peaceful oasis in its centre. Now walk through Judengasse – a mecca for fashion lovers with all of its small boutiques – until you reach Hoher Markt → p. 36. Make a detour through Salvatorgasse to visit the church Maria am Gestade → p. 39, a gem of Gothic archi-

If you feel that the time has now come for a short shopping spree, we recommend the adjacent Kohlmarkt, probably Vienna's most elegant consumer paradise. But, you should really head in the opposite direction towards Hofburg → p. 35; first of all beneath the massive verdigris-covered dome of the Michaelertor to the Innerer Burghof. The entrance to the Kaiserappartements → p. 36 with the official and private rooms of Emperor Franz Joseph and his wife Elisabeth – the Sisi Museum → p. 36 is devoted entirely to her – is on the rights in the so-called Reichskanzleitrakt. The same staircase takes you to the fascinating Silberkammer. Walk through the shopping arcade in the southeast corner of the courtyard and you will soon find yourself on Heldenplatz → p. 34. Here, on this enormous open space, you will really feel the atmosphere of the former Habsburg Empire. The silhouettes of some of the most famous buildings on the Ringstraße lie in front of you: Parlament → p. 42 to the northwest with the Rathaus → p. 41 behind it; the Palace of Justice lies to the left of the parliament building and the Naturhistorisches Museum → p. 41 and the Kunsthistorisches Museum → p. 37 dominate the southwest behind the fortress-like Outer Palace Gate that was originally erected as a monument to the Battle of Leipzig. The Leopoldine Tract, where Austria's president has his residence, is just behind you. The enormous semicircle to the east is the Neue Hofburg. It houses several extremely interesting museums – the Museum of Ethnology and the Ephesus Museum, as well as collections of weapons and old musical instruments. A Congress Centre is located in the left wing – it is hard to imagine any other city having a more exquisite site for meetings. This setting with elaborate stucco work and state-of-the-art technology has helped cement Vienna's reputation as a leading metropolis for international diplomacy.

COFFEEHOUSE TOUR AROUND THE OPERA HOUSE AND HOFBURG

This tour is something for coffee junkies and will take you to some ● coffeehouses where European intellectual history was written. The area around the Naschmarkt and the spectacular buildings in the western section of the Old Town are a feast for the eyes. Depending on how often you stop for refreshments, the walk will take between two and five hours.

Is it possible to imagine a more atmospheric way to start the day than with a *Melange mit Schlag* (coffee with milk and whipped cream) at one of the little marble tables in Sperl → p. 67 at Gumpendorfer Straße 11? Once you have had your

fill on one of the plush benches underneath the chandeliers in this famous café, which has been filmed and photographed so often, saunter down to Lehárgasse and then past the historical Theater an der Wien until you reach Naschmarkt → p. 78. Here, in the 'belly of Vienna', you can go explore the stands with their pyramids of fruit and vegetables, sausages and cheese, and sushi and kebab restaurants.

After this, cross over to the Secession → p. 44 with its Jugendstil dome of golden leaves at the western tip of Karlsplatz. The Café Museum (*daily | Operngasse 7*) on the corner of Operngasse and Karlsplatz was originally decorated by nobody less than Adolf Loos. The café recently reopened after extensive renovations to restore it to its original state and will tempt you to make another short break. You should at least take a quick look inside. Now turn your gaze to the right towards the Baroque dome of Karlskirche → p. 52 before strolling along the outer section of Kärntner Straße and over the Ring to the Staatsoper → p. 45, 87. The cosy, comparatively new, Café Oper Wien (*daily*) next to the well-stocked Arcadia music shop might seem to be an inviting place to take a rest but two very famous traditional cafés behind the temple of the Muses will probably appeal too: Sacher (*daily | Philharmonikerstraße 4*) on the ground floor of the hotel of the same name where you will not be able to avoid having a slice of the legendary chocolate cake and, just around the corner, the hardly less elegant Café Mozart (*daily | Albertinaplatz 2*. Cross the road and walk past the Albertina → p. 29, Alfred Hrdlicka's Monument against War and Fascism → p. 39 and Palais Lobkowitz until you reach the Dorotheum → p. 75 auction house. The Bräunerhof (*daily | Stallburggasse 2*) used to be the favourite café of Austria's main literary grumbler Thomas Bernhard and is now your next stop. Go around the corner and, diagonally opposite the Judisches Museum → p. 36, you will land in one of the hotspots of intellectual protest in the 1950s and '60s: the artists' café Hawelka (Wed–Mon | Dorotheergasse 6). Maybe you should try a *buchtel* – a warm yeast dumpling filled with jam and served with vanilla sauce. These were the speciality of Josefine Hawelka whose husband, Leopold, made sure the tradition was continued after her death until he died in 2011 at the age of 100. Well fortified, it's time for a complete change of scene – from the home-away-from-home of Vienna's Bohemians to the incomparably elegant Café Demel (daily | Kohlmarkt 12). The white-aproned waitresses tempt guests to sin against any dietary resolutions they might have made when they show them all of the luxurious delicacies in the glass showcases. It is only a few steps from here past a row of new luxury boutiques to Griensteidl (daily | Michaelerplatz 2). This is where Karl Kraus and Egon Erwin Kisch fought battles with their pens at the start of the 20th century, and where Hugo von Hofmannsthal, Franz Werfel and Joseph Roth polished their literary works. The future of the world's literature and politics was largely determined under the high vaults of the Café Central → p. 65 only a five-minute walk away at Herrengasse 14. Today's tourists are probably more interested in the magnificent atmosphere of this café in Palais Ferstel → p. 42.

3 KAHLENBERG AND LEOPOLDSBERG

It is not difficult to reach these two ✴ hills so popular among the Viennese – just catch bus 38A at Heiligenstadt underground station (U4, U6); you also take the same route via Grinzing if you drive out from the city centre. The most beautiful path for hikers leads from Grinzing to Kahlenberg and then on to Leopoldsberg (142–143 C–D2) (𝄞 0) in around two hours.

The panoramic views make this excursion a real treat. There are wonderful vistas of Vienna and the Vienna Basin as far as the Leitha Mountains and Slovakian Carpathians from the two 'summits'. If you take the bus, you will reach the terminus in the valley after around 20 minutes. However, if you want to climb Vienna's local mountains 'on Shanks's pony', you should take tram 38 to the terminus (or bus 38A to the Grinzing/Sandgasse stop). From there, head to the north up Grinzinger Steig to Heiligenstadt Cemetery; turn left and follow Wildgrubgasse along the Schreiberbach through the Mukental. Finally, after a little more than half a mile, turn right up a long flight of steps at the

end of which you will find several signposts to guide you safely through the woods to **Kahlenberg**.

By the way, this imposing 484m (1588ft)-high hill in the woods was called Sauberg (Pig Mountain) until the late 18th century on account of the many wild boar. At the time, it was the neighbouring peak, 60m (200ft) lower, that was called Kahlenberg. However, when a church was built there in 1683 to honour the reigning Emperor Leopold I, the site was given the name of the illustrious Kaiser – and the Sauberg was rechristened Kahlenberg. The trendy INSIDER TIP *CoffeeToGo (daily 7am–5pm | tel. 06 64 2 13 20 91)* with its three terraces, winter garden, deckchairs and fabulous view over Vienna will certainly tempt you to stop and have some delicious cake and organic coffee.

A pleasant footpath takes you from Kahlenberg to **Leopoldsberg** in under half an hour, where you will be able to admire the two-towered façade of the small **Leopoldskirche** in the middle of the ruins of a Babenberg fortress from the 13th century. After this, take a bus or drive along the Höhenstraße, a panoramic road through the Vienna Woods built in the 1930s as an employment scheme. Side roads lead down to the *Heurigen* districts of Sievering, Neustift, Pötzleinsdorf and Salmannsdorf. A must: stop at the **Lebenbaumkreis am Himmel**, a unique natural monument *(www.himmel.at)* laid out as an acoustic space where, in the afternoons at weekends, you can listen to classical music or jazz from 40 loudspeakers and enjoy the unparalleled view of Vienna – all free of charge. Take bus 38A to the Cobenzl stop and walk for around 10 mins. along Höhenstraße towards Sievering until you reach the corner of Himmelstraße and Höhenstraße.

Twilight atmosphere on Kahlenberg: the reward for the long ascent is a visit to a *Heuriger*

TRAVEL WITH KIDS

DSCHUNGEL WIEN
(126 A–B 4–5) (*ญ J9*)

Located next to the Zoom Kindermuseum, this theatre holds plays, dance, pantomime and puppet performances focusing on the very young (18 months) to young at heart 25-year-olds. *Museumsplatz 1 | tel. 5 22 07 20 | www.dschungelwien.at | bus 2 A, U2 Museumsquartier*

FIGURENTHEATER LILARUM
(135 D2) (*ญ N9*)

Glove and rod puppets lead children from 3–8 years into the realm of fantasy. Here, they can make 'cloud sheep' and 'plant charmers' their friends. *Göllnergasse 8 | tel. 7 10 26 66 | www.lilarum.at | bus 77A, U3 Kardinal Nagl-Platz*

HAUS DES MEERES (138 C2) (*ญ H10*)

Domestic and tropical freshwater and saltwater fish – as well as poisonous and gigantic snakes, lizards and crocodiles – live in Esterházypark. Children can watch sharks and piranhas being fed and pat turtles. Brightly-coloured exotic birds fly through the air in the Tropical Building and little monkeys might even jump onto your shoulder. *Daily 9am–6pm, Thu 9pm | children 6–15 years: 5.90, under 6: 4 euros, adults: 12.90 euros | Fritz-Grünbaum-Platz 1 | www.haus-des-meeres.at | U3 Neubaugasse, bus 13A, 14A Haus des Meeres*

KINDER UND JUGENDKINO
(137 D6) (*ญ K9*)

Cinemagic is special cinema for young film fans from the age of 3. All kinds of films are shown – from funny cartoons to prize-winning productions for kids and teenagers. The highlight is the annual International Children's Film Festival in mid-November. *Friedrichstraße 4 | tel. 4 00 08 34 00 | tram 1, 2, D, 62, 65, bus 59A, U1, U2, U4 Karlsplatz*

INSIDER TIP MINOPOLIS
(131 E6) (*ญ P5*)

Europe's first and only big city scaled down for children. 4–12-year-olds learn how to deal with money and the ins-and-outs of more than 100 professions at more than 25 carefully created thematic centres under the guidance of 80 trained coaches. *July/ Aug Wed–Sat 1pm–7pm, Sept–June Fri– Sun 1pm–7pm | children 19 euros, parents*

'Cloud sheep' and imperial children: Vienna has a great range of leisure and cultural events on offer for young people

10 euros | Wagramer Straße 2 | Cineplexx Reichsbrücke | tel. 08 10 97 02 70 | www.minopolis.at | U1 Donauinsel

SCHÖNBRUNN FÜR KIDS
(136 A–C 4–6) (*∭ D12*)

6–12-year-olds can find out about the state rooms on special tours for children (*Sat, Sun 2.30pm | children 5.50, adults 7 euros*). The palace ghost tells all kinds of interesting things about the everyday life of the imperial children in the *Kindermuseum (Sat, Sun, public and school holidays, 10am–5pm | children 5.50, adults 7 euros*). There are many funny and unusual games in the *Labyrinthikon. www.kaiserkinder.at | U4 Schönbrunn or Hietzing*

WIENXTRA-KINDERINFO
The information office provides details on special theatre activities for kids, game parties, party ships, nature excursions, etc. *Tue–Thu 2pm–7pm, Fri–Sun 10am–5pm | Museumsquartier/Hof 2 | Museumsplatz 1 | tel. 4 00 08 44 00 | www.wienxtra.at | bus 2A, U2 Museumsquartier*

ZOOM KINDERMUSEUM
(126 A–B 4–5) (*∭ J9*)

The MuseumsQuartier also has a special museum for children, with *Ozean*, a waterbed-tunnel-landscape (for babies and children under 3) and a studio for budding artists (aged 3–12), to a multimedia laboratory where you can experiment with animated films, sound and 3D spaces (ages 8–14). Set starting times for all events; reservation advisable! *Tel. information Mon–Fri 8am–4pm, Sat, Sun 9am–4pm | entrance fee for children plus one adult, 5 euros, family ticket (max. two adults and three children) 12 euros | Museumsplatz 1 | tel. 5 24 79 08 | www.kindermuseum.at | bus 2A, U2 Museumsquartier*

FESTIVALS & EVENTS

From the New Year's Concert to the Festival Weeks and the Film Viennale to the ball season, life is never boring in Vienna.

PUBLIC HOLIDAYS

1 Jan New Year, **6 Jan** Epiphany, Easter Monday, **1 May** Labour Day, **Ascension**, **Whit Monday**, **Corpus Christi**, **15 Aug** Assumption, **26 Oct** National Holiday, **1 Nov** All Saints', **8 Dec** Immaculate Conception, **25/26 Dec** Christmas

EVENTS

JANUARY/FEBRUARY

1 Jan: ▶ *New Year's Concert* by the Vienna Philharmonic in the Golden Hall of the Musikverein (127 D6) (*L9*), tel. 5 05 65 25. **INSIDER TIP** Internet lottery for tickets in Jan, 1 year in advance, under *www.wienerphilharmoniker.at*
Beginning of Jan–late Feb: ▶ *Carnival and ball season*. More than 200 festive balls in spectacular settings
2nd half of Jan: ▶ *Resonanzen*. Festival of old music. Konzerthaus (127 E6) (*L9*), tickets tel. 24 20 02, *www.konzerthaus.at*

MARCH–MAY

Holy Week/Easter weekend: ▶ *Oster-Klang*. Top-class musicians including the Vienna Philharmonic play solemn and festive works, tickets tel. 588 85
Mid-April–early May: ▶ *Spring Festival* in the Konzerthaus (127 E6) (*L9*). Classical music, tickets tel. 24 20 02

APRIL–JUNE

▶ *Vienna Spring Marathon*. Race from Reichsbrücke to Heldenplatz. Tel. 6 06 95 10, *www.vienna-marathon.com*
Early May–mid-June: ▶ *Wiener Festwochen*. Cutting-edge theatrical art from around the world performed at dozens of locations. Advanced bookings: Wiener Festwochen, A-1060 Wien, Lehárgasse 11, tel. 5 89 22 22, with credit card: 5 89 22 11, *www.festwochen.at*
End of May: ▶ *Lifeball*. Europe's largest Aids charity event with a high celebrity count and a spectacular, show open to all in front of the Town Hall (126 A–B 2–3) (*J8*). Tel. 5 95 56 00, *www.lifeball.org*
Last weekend in June: ▶ *Donauinselfest* (130–131 A1–E6) (*L1–S9*) – three-day party with music, shows and cabaret

Mega-parties, the marathon and music festivals – it is always high season in Vienna with something of interest for everyone

JULY–SEPTEMBER

Beginning of July: ▶ *Jazzfest*. In the streets, clubs and the Opera (126 C5) (*K9*), tickets tel. 7 12 42 24, www.viennajazz.org
Beginning of July–mid-Aug: ▶ *ImPulsTanz – Vienna International Dance Festival*. Body art in its most perfect form, tickets tel. 5 23 55 58, www.impulstanz.com
July, Aug: ▶ INSIDER TIP *Musikfilmfestival* in front of the Town Hall (126 A–B 2–3) (*J8*), www.wien-event.at
July–early Sept: ▶ *Klangbogen Wien*. 150 operettas, operas, orchestra and chamber-music concerts at beautiful locations, ticket tel. 5 88 85, www.theater-wien.at

OCTOBER

▶ *Lange Nacht der Museen*. 90 museums open to 1am, with a single ticket
▶ *Viennale*. The latest cinematic creations from around the world, tel. 52 65 94 70, www.viennale.at

End of Oct–end of Nov: ▶ *Wien modern*. Music of the 20th and 21st centuries in the Musikverein (127 D6) (*L9*) and Konzerthaus (127 E6) (*L9*), tel. 24 20 02 and 5 05 81 90, www.wienmodern.at

NOVEMBER

2nd week in Nov in the Hofburg (126 B–C 3–4) (*K 8–9*): ▶ *Internationale Kunst- und Antiquitätenmesse Wien*, www.kunstmessewien.at

DECEMBER

▶ *27 Advent Markets*
31 Dec: The ▶ INSIDER TIP *Silvesterpfad* (New Year's Eve Path) winds its way through the entire Inner City. With many booths, sideshow attractions, stages for music performances and tents for dancing. The highlight comes at midnight when the Pummerin in St Stephen's, rings in the New Year (127 D3) (*L8*), www.silvesterpfad.at

LINKS, BLOGS, APPS & MORE

LINKS

▶ www.wien.gv.at/tourismus Comprehensive information on life in the city on this user-friendly website: leisure, culture, sport, food & drink, sightseeing and much more. The virtual walks make it possible for you to experience all this in the comfort of your own home

▶ www.gespenster.at Those who are interested in taking a somewhat different kind of tour and be scared out of their wits should register for this spirit, ghost and vampire tour through Vienna

▶ http://aboutvienna.org Everything at a glance: maps, best addresses, what to do and where to go, and even where to learn German

▶ www.wienerleben.at For those who are not so courageous, this site offers an overview of guided tours dealing with everyday culture in Vienna from the cofeehouse to the fiacre; plus useful links to Viennese apartments, educational tours and more

NETWORK

▶ www.lonelyplanet.com/thorntree/forum.jspa?forumID=27&keywordid=106 The Thorntree Forum of the Lonely Planet Community is the place where former and future visitors to Vienna can exchange information: most of the entries are in English

▶ vivirbien.mediavirus.org/resources/view/all ⏱ The layout resembles Google Maps but this charts solidarity projects and cooperatives in Vienna. You will find it easy to locate organic ice-cream shops, autonomous cafés, places to go swimming and shops where you can exchange things or even get them for free

Regardless of whether you are still preparing your trip or already in Vienna: these addresses will provide you with more information, videos and networks to make your holiday even more enjoyable

NETWORK

▶ twitter.com/RadioArabella Vienna's best-known radio station twitters the latest information on politics and culture, but more profane things such as the weather and city traffic are also given their due

▶ www.wien.info/en Very helpful forum for tourists and other newcomers to the city; the topics range from restaurant tips, places to go out to in the evening, to public transport

BLOGS

▶ www.expat-blog.com/en/directory/europe/austria/vienna Blogs written by expats living in Vienna for those thinking of working, living or moving to Vienna. Or if you just want to find out more about life in Austria's capital

▶ www.thebestofviennablog.com An ever-expanding network aimed at highlighting the city's most appealing assets, its cosmopolitan and multi-cultural lifestyle, etc.

VIDEOS

▶ http://vimeo.com/17963614 Time-lapse impressions of the city that are given a starkly surrealistic effect through the colourations; unfortunately, only about 90 seconds long

▶ www.youtube.com/watch?v=OMrwcix41sY It is impossible to think of Vienna without its musical ambassador Falco; here, he sings about *Viennese Blood* – and gallons of it flow in this video. Not only his fish tie makes this a gem of 1980s trash culture

APPS

▶ www.tripwolf.com/en/page/iphone The free Vienna app from tripwolf is particularly well suited for short trips to the Danube metropolis but there are enough tips and information for longer stays. It is even equipped with augmented-reality elements

TRAVEL TIPS

ARRIVAL

✈ There are many non-stop flights daily to Vienna, operated by British Airways, British Midland, Easyjet, Austrian, Lufthansa, and other carriers, from airports in London and other cities in the UK. Vienna's International Airport is located in Schwechat 15km (9½mi) southeast of the city centre. Buses connect the airport with the railway stations *(7 euros | approx. 30 min)* and there is a City Airport Train (CAT) every half hour directly to Wien–Mitte *(12 euros | online 9 euros | 16 min | www.cityairporttrain.com)*. A more economic alternative is the S-Bahn, S7, S2, every thirty minutes; however, there are many stops on the way *(4 euros | half-price with the Wien-Karte | close to 30 min.)*.

BANKS & CREDIT CARDS

Bank opening hours: *Mon–Wed and Fri 8am–3pm | Thu 8am–5.30pm | many local branches have a lunch break from 12.30–1.30pm.* Standard credit cards are usually accepted. Reports of loss and queries: *American Express tel. 51 51 10 | Airplus/Diners Club tel. 50 13 50 | MasterCard tel. 71 70 10 | Visa tel. 7 11 11*

BICYCLE HIRE

You can take a *Citybike* from any one of the 80 bases throughout Vienna at any time of the day or night. This is free of charge and you do not have to return the bike to where you started. *www.citybikewien.at*

CITY TOURS

By tram: around the Ringstraße on the Ring Tram; you can get on or of at any stop. *Year round, daily 10am–6pm | departure from Schwedenplatz 10 mins. before and 20 past the hour; first departure at 10 am from the Staatsoper | duration: approx. 25 mins., 6 euros; 9 euros for 24 hours*
On four wheels: in a chauffeured vintage car through the city and out into the countryside. Set, or individual, routes and durations. *Tel. 06 64 4 11 88 93 | www.oldiefahrt.at*
On two wheels: guided bicycle tours lasting 2–3 hours: *Bike & Guide (tel. 06 99 11 75 82 61 | www.bikeandguide.com)* and *Pedal Power (Ausstellungsstr. 3 (134 C3) (ΩΩ N7) | tel. 7 29 72 34 | www.pedalpower. at).* Free information and sale of bike maps and literature also from: *ARBÖ (Mariahilfer Straße 180 (137 E3) (ΩΩ F11) | tel. 89 12 17)* and *ARGUS (Frankenberggasse 11 (139 E2) (ΩΩ J10) | tel. 5 05 09 07).*
By bus: *Vienna Sightseeing Tours (tel. 7 12 46 8 30 | www.viennasightseeing.at), Red Bus City Tours (Tel. 5 12 40 30)* and

RESPONSIBLE TRAVEL

It doesn't take a lot to be environmentally friendly whilst travelling. Don't just think about your carbon footprint whilst flying to and from your holiday destination but also about how you can protect nature and culture abroad. As a tourist it is especially important to respect nature, look out for local products, cycle instead of driving, save water and much more. If you would like to find out more about eco-tourism please visit: *www.ecotourism.org*

From arrival to weather

Cityrama (Tel. 5 04 75 00) organise several tours of the city every day. The buses of the *Vienna Line Hop On Hop Off* run between 15 stations on 3 set routes daily every hour *(Mon–Thu 10am–5pm, Fri–Sun 10.30am–4.40pm)*. With a day ticket for 20 euros (children 7 euros) you can get on and off as you wish. The central station is in front of the Staatsoper. Alternative bus tours (and also by bike) on special aspects of Vienna are organised by the *Stattwerkstatt | Kolingasse 6 (126 B1) (*∭ J7) | Tel. 3 19 86 66.*

By motorboat: *(only May–Oct): DDSG Blue Danube Schifffahrt | Friedrichstr. 7 | tel. 58 88 00 | www.ddsg-blue-danube.at* On foot: The *Vienna Guide Service (Sommerhaidenweg 124 | tel. 7 86 24 00 | www.viennaguideservice.com)* arranges individual tours; half day approx. 120 euros, full day (up to 6 hours) around 240 euros. A group of professional tourist guides offers 'Walks in Vienna' on specific subjects (14 euros per person). Monthly list of tours from information offices *(tel. 4 89 96 74 | www.wienguide.at)*.

CONSULATES & EMBASSIES

BRITISH EMBASSY
Jauresgasse 12 | 1030 Vienna | tel.: +43 171 6130 | viennaconsularenquiries@fco.gov.uk

EMBASSY OF THE UNITED STATES OF AMERICA
Boltzmanngasse 16 | 1090 Vienna | tel.: +43 13 13 33 90 | austria.usembassy.gov

EMBASSY OF CANADA
Laurenzerberg 2 | 1010 Vienna | tel.: +43 15 31 38 30 00 | www.canadainternational.gc.ca/austria-autriche

CUSTOMS

The regulations governing the European single market apply to dealings with other EU countries: goods for private consumption are tax-free; including 800 cigarettes, 10 litres of spirits, 90 litres of wine and 110 litres of beer.

BUDGETING

Taxi	£1/$1.70 *per kilometre, during the day*
Coffee	£2.15/$3.50 *for an espresso*
Parking	50p/¢80 *for 30 minutes*
Wine	£2.40/$3.90 *for a glass (0.125 l)*
Theatre ticket	from £6.40/$10.50
Snack	Around £2/$3.30 *for frankfurters at a sausage stand*

DRIVING

The traffic regulations in Austria are similar to those in most other European countries. It is compulsory for drivers to wear seatbelts and have high visibility jackets in the car in the case of a breakdown; winter tyres are obligatory Nov–March and motorcyclists must wear a helmet. The legal drink-driving limit is 0.5%. The speed limit on motorways is 130 km/h (80mph), on main roads 100 km/h (60mph) and 50km/h (30mph) in built up areas. Breakdown assistance: *ÖAMTC | tel. 120,* and *ARBÖ | tel. 1 23.*

During the day, parking is only allowed with a parking ticket in many Viennese districts. There are several underground car parks in the city centre. You can obtain a free brochure with information on parking in Vienna (short-term, permanent and overnight parking, park & ride, garages, etc) from *www.parkeninwien.at* under the key word: *Parkfibel*.

equestrian statues (126 B4) (*Ⓜ K8*) and on the north side of the cathedral on Stephansplatz (127 D3) (*Ⓜ L8*).

INFORMATION BEFORE YOUR DEPARTURE

AUSTRIAN NATIONAL TOURIST OFFICE
www.austria.info/uk; telephone UK: 08451011818; Ireland: 1890930118

EMERGENCY SERVICES

24-hour chemists: *tel. 1550;* emergency doctor: *tel. 141;* fire brigade: *tel. 122;* police: *tel. 133;* ambulance: *tel. 144;* night dentist: *tel. 5122078*

INFORMATION IN VIENNA

WIEN-TOURISMUS
Daily 9am–7pm | 1010 | Albertinaplatz/ corner Maysedergasse (126 C5) (Ⓜ K9) | tel. 24555 | daily 6am–11pm in the arrivals hall at the airport | tel. 700701 | www. wien.info

FIACRE

Sitting comfortably in a ● horse-drawn carriage is a stylish way to become acquainted with the beauty of Vienna. A 1-hour city tour costs approx. 95 euros (agree on the price before you start!); a shorter 20-minute ride is about 40 euros. All of the fiacre ranks are in the First District: on Augustinerstraße in front of the Albertina **(126 C4)** (*Ⓜ K9*), on Heldenplatz on the road between the two

WIEN XTRA JUGEND- UND KINDER-INFO (126 B5) (*Ⓜ K9*)
Information for Children and Young People: Advice and tickets for anyone up to the age of 26. *Youth information: Mon– Wed 2pm–7pm, Thu–Sat 1pm–6pm | 1010 | Babenbergerstraße/corner Burgring | tel. 4000 84100 | www.jugendinfowien.at |*

VOICES OF GOLD

The Vienna Boys' Choir, accompanied by members of the chorus and orchestra of the Staatsloper, performs at mass in the Burgkapelle in the Hofburg (entrance: Schweizerhof) every Sun from mid-Sept to the end of June and on Christmas Day. Mass starts at 9.15am. Written ticket requests must be sent at least 10 weeks in advance to *Hofmusikkapelle | A-1010 Wien | Hofburg | tel. +431 5339927 | whmk@chello.at*. Any remaining seats can be purchased at the box office near the Chapel *(Fri 11am–1pm and 3pm– 5pm, Sat from 8.15am)*. In addition, the Boys' Choir performs Strauss melodies and works from the Romantic period in the Musikverein at 4pm on Fri from mid-April to June and again in Sept and Oct. Tickets available in hotels or from *Reisebüro Mondial | tel. +431 58804173 | www.mondial.at*. General information on the Choir: *www.wsk.at*

Children information: in MuseumsQuartier/ Hof 2 | Tue–Thu 2pm–7pm, Fri–Sun 10am–5pm | tel. 4 00 08 44 00 | www.kinderinfo wien.at

INTERNET CAFÉS & WI-FI

Many cafés and institutions provide free wireless Internet access. You can download a listing of the more than 300 hotspots under *www.freewave.at. Multi Media Stations* at more than 500 locations available to the public make it possible to access the City of Vienna's sites, including tourist information, free of charge. In addition, you can also make free calls to the service sections of the city administration from the stations. If you insert the right coins, you will also be able to telephone, surf in the Internet, send text messages and e-mails and make video calls.

PHONE & MOBILE PHONE

Phonecards for public card telephones are available from tobacconists and post offices (5, 10 or 20 euros). It is advisable to buy a prepaid card in Vienna for your mobile phone to save costs on incoming calls. The major providers are *A 1 (www. a1.net), One (www.orange.at), T-Mobile (www.t-mobile.at), Hutchinson 3 (www. drei.at)*. Texting is an economical alternative to telephoning. Your mailbox can be very costly: turning it off is a good idea! The international dialling code for Austria is: *0043*, the area code for Vienna: *(0)1*. Dial *0044* for the UK followed by the area code without the *0*, and *001* for the USA and Canada.

POST

Opening times usually *Mon–Fri 8am–noon and 2pm–6pm (cash desks to 5pm)*, main

Fiacre outside the Hofburg

district post offices *Mon–Fri 8am–6pm*, Main Post Office **(127 E3)** *(⋒ L8) Mon–Fri 7am–10pm, Sat, Sun 9am–10pm | Fleischmarkt 19 | U4 Schwedenplatz*; Westbahnhof **(137 F2)** *(⋒ G10) Mon–Fri 7am–10pm, Sat, Sun 9am–10pm | Europaplatz 1 | U3, U6 Westbahnhof*

PUBLIC TRANSPORT

Vienna has 5 underground lines (they operate approx. 5am–0.30am with 24-hour service on Fri and Sat and and the night before public holidays), several suburban railway lines (S-Bahn) and countless tram, bus and night-bus lines. Tickets can be purchased at tobacconists and from machines at underground stations; tickets for the night bus can be bought on the bus. If purchased in advance, a ticket for bus, underground, tram or suburban railway (to the city border) costs 2 euros or else 2.20 euros from the conductor. The *Klimakarte* (valid on 8 individual days) costs 33.80 euros and there are also 24hour tickets (4.90 euros – purchase via mobile phone!), 48 hours (11.70 euros) and one calendar week (15 euros). Children under 6 travel free of charge, as do those up to 15 on Sun and

now consists mainly of low-level vehicles without steps. The suburban railway is not quite so advanced. Special maps of the city provide information for wheelchair users: available from *Wiener Tourismusverband (tel. 2 11 11 42 22)*.

The *Wien-Karte (Vienna Card)* (19.90 euros) entitles holders to unlimited use of all public transportation within the city boundary for 72 hours and also includes reductions to most museums and sights and many other extras. Children und the age of 15 and senior citizens can possibly save even more if they take advantage of the various reductions. Don't forget your passport for identification! The *Wien-Karte* can be obtained in more than 200 hotels, at tourist information offices and all major sales offices of the Viennese public transport organisation. Or you can order the ticket before you leave home *(tel. 7 98 40 01 48 | www.wienkarte.at)*. *Information centres for the Wiener Linien at Stephansplatz, Karlsplatz/Passage, Westbahnhof and several other locations| Mon–Fri 6.30am–6.30pm, Sat, Sun 8.30am–4pm | tel. 7 90 91 00 | www.wienerlinien.at.*

CURRENCY CONVERTER

£	€	€	£
1	1.30	1	0.80
3	3.80	3	2.40
5	6.30	5	4
13	16.30	13	10
40	50	40	32
75	94	75	60
120	150	120	96
250	313	250	200
500	625	500	400

$	€	€	$
1	0.80	1	1.30
3	2.30	3	3.90
5	3.80	5	6.50
13	10	13	11
40	30.80	40	52
75	58	75	98
120	92	120	156
250	192	250	325
500	385	500	650

For current exchange rates see www.xe.com

public holidays and during school breaks (ID necessary!). 24-hour information for excursions by train in the immediate area of Vienna: *tel. 0 51 71 73*

There are lifts in most underground stations and almost all vehicles have lowered doors and sufficient space. The transportation fleet is currently being converted and

SMOKING

Although cigarettes have already been banned from government buildings and public institutions and most hotels are now nicotine-free, a law stipulates that restaurant owners must display clearly if their establishment is a 'smoking' or 'non-smoking' environment or have at least two separate sections (see signs at the entrances).

TAXIS

Radio taxis *tel. 3 13 00, tel. 4 01 00, tel. 6 01 60, tel. 8 14 00*. Fares for journeys outside the city limits should be agreed on in advance.

TICKETS

Tickets for federal theatres (Staatsoper, Volksoper, Burgtheater, Akademietheater) can be ordered in advance in writing from *Bundestheater | A-1010 Wien | Operngasse 2* . Tickets for the entire coming season in the Staatsoper go on sale immediately after the programme is announced in March/April. Sales and remaining tickets in the Bundestheater box office, online under *www.culturall.com* and with credit card under *tel. 5 13 15 13*. Information *tel. 5 14 44 78 80* or *www.artforart.at*

Wien-Ticket is the organisation responsible for tickets to the Theater an der Wien, Ronacher, Raimundtheater and all of the other WVS venues. *Central box office: Wien-Ticket Pavilion next to the State Opera | daily 10am–7pm | credit-card bookings tel. 5 88 85 (daily 9am–9pm) | www.wien-ticket.at*

Tickets on the internet: *www.culturall. com* and *www.viennaticketoffice.com*

TIME

Vienna is one hour ahead of Greenwich Mean Time and six hours ahead of US Eastern Time.

TIPPING

Waiters/taxi drivers 5–10%, room service 1–2 euros/day, porters 50 cents–1.50 euros.

WEATHER

Vienna has a moderate continental climate. This means: cold winters, hot relatively dry summers and rain in spring and autumn. The best time to visit the city is in late spring or early autumn. Weather forecast: *www.orf.at/wetter*

WEATHER IN VIENNA

	Jan	Feb	March	April	May	June	July	Aug	Sept	Oct	Nov	Dec
Daytime temperatures in °C/°F	1/34	3/37	8/46	14/57	19/66	22/72	25/77	24/75	20/68	14/57	7/45	3/37
Nighttime temperatures in °C/°F	−4/25	−2/28	1/34	6/43	10/50	13/55	15/59	15/59	11/52	7/45	3/37	−1/30
Sunshine hours/day	2	3	4	6	7	8	8	8	7	5	2	1
Precipitation days/month	8	7	8	8	9	9	9	9	7	8	8	8

USEFUL PHRASES GERMAN

PRONUNCIATION

We have provided a simple pronunciation aid for the german words
(see the square brackets). Note the following:

ch	usually like ch in Scottish "loch", shown here as [kh]
g	hard as in "get"
ß	is a double s
ä	like the vowel in "fair" or "bear"
ö	a little like er as in "her"
ü	is spoken as ee with rounded lips, like the French "tu"
ie	is ee as in "fee", but ei is like "height", shown here as [ei]
'	stress on the following syllable

IN BRIEF

Yes/No/Maybe	Ja [yah]/Nein [nein]/Vielleicht [fee'leikht]
Please/Thank you	Bitte ['bi-te]/Danke ['dan-ke]
Sorry	Entschuldige [ent'shul-di-ge]
Excuse me, please	Entschuldigen Sie [ent'shul-di-gen zee]
May I ...?/ Pardon?	Darf ich ...? [darf ikh]/Wie bitte? [vee 'bi-te]
I would like to .../	Ich möchte ... [ikh 'merkh-te]/
have you got ...?	Haben Sie ...? ['hab-en zee]
How much is ...?	Wie viel kostet ...? [vee-feel 'koss-tet]
I (don't) like this	Das gefällt mir/nicht [das ge-'felt meer/nikht]
good/bad	gut/schlecht [goot/shlekht]
broken/doesn't work	kaputt [ka-'put]/funktioniert nicht/
	funk-tsion-'eert nikht]
too much/much/little	(zu) viel/wenig [tsoo feel/'vay-nikh]
Help!/Attention!/ Caution!	Hilfe! ['hil-fe]/Achtung! [akh-'tung]/ Vorsicht! ['for-sikht]
ambulance	Krankenwagen ['kran-ken-vaa-gen]/
	Notarzt ['note-aatst]
police/fire brigade	Polizei [pol-i-'tsei]/Feuerwehr ['foy-er-vayr]
danger/dangerous	Gefahr [ge-'far]/gefährlich [ge-'fair-likh]

GREETINGS, FAREWELL

Good morning!/after-	Gute(n) Morgen ['goo-ten 'mor-gen]/Tag [taag]/
noon!/evening!/night!	Abend ['aa-bent]/Nacht [nakht]
Hello!/goodbye!	Hallo ['ha-llo]/Auf Wiedersehen [owf 'vee-der-zayn]

Sprichst du Deutsch?

"Do you speak German?" This guide will help you to say the basic words and phrases in German.

See you!	Tschüss [chüss]
My name is ...	Ich heiße ... [ikh 'hei-sse]
What's your name?	Wie heißt Du [vee heist doo]/ heißen Sie? ['heiss-en zee]
I'm from ...	Ich komme aus ... [ikh 'ko-mme ows]

DATE & TIME

Monday/Tuesday	Montag ['moan-tag]/Dienstag ['deens-tag]
Wednesday/Thursday	Mittwoch ['mit-vokh]/Donnerstag ['don-ers-tag]
Friday/Saturday	Freitag ['frei-tag]/Samstag ['zams-tag]
Sunday/holiday	Sonntag ['zon-tag]/Feiertag ['fire-tag]
today/tomorrow/ yesterday	heute ['hoy-te]/morgen ['mor-gen]/ gestern ['gess-tern]
hour/minute	Stunde ['shtun-de]/Minute [min-'oo-le]
day/night/week	Tag [tag]/Nacht [nakht]/Woche ['vo-khe]
What time is it?	Wie viel Uhr ist es? ['vee-feel oor ist es]
It's three o'clock	Es ist drei Uhr [ez ist drei oor]

TRAVEL

open/closed	offen ['off-en]/geschlossen [ge-'shloss-en]
entrance (vehicles)	Zufahrt ['tsoo-faat]
entrance/exit	Eingang ['ein-gang]/Ausgang ['ows-gang]
arrival/departure (flight)	Ankunft ['an-kunft]/Abflug ['ap-floog]
toilets/restrooms / ladies/gentlemen	Toiletten [twa-'let-en]/ Damen ['daa-men]/Herren ['her-en]
(no) drinking water	(kein) Trinkwasser [(kein) 'trink-vass-er]
Where is ...?/Where are ...?	Wo ist ...? [vo ist]/Wo sind ...? [vo zint]
left/right	links [links]/rechts [rekhts]
straight ahead/back	geradeaus [ge-raa-de-'ows]/zurück [tsoo-'rük]
close/far	nah [naa]/weit [veit]
taxi/cab	Taxi ['tak-si]
bus stop/ cab stand	Bushaltestelle [bus-hal-te-'shtell-e]/ Taxistand ['tak-si- shtant]
parking lot/parking garage	Parkplatz ['park-plats]/Parkhaus ['park-hows]
street map/map	Stadtplan ['shtat-plan]/Landkarte ['lant-kaa-te]
airport/train station	Flughafen ['floog-ha-fen]/ Bahnhof ['baan-hoaf]
schedule/ticket	Fahrplan ['faa-plan]/Fahrschein ['faa-shein]
I would like to rent ...	Ich möchte ... mieten [ikh 'mer-khte ... 'mee-ten]
a car/a bicycle	ein Auto [ein 'ow-to]/ein Fahrrad [ein 'faa-raat]
a motorhome/RV	ein Wohnmobil [ein 'vone-mo-beel]
a boat	ein Boot [ein 'boat]

petrol/gas station	Tankstelle ['tank-shtell-e]
petrol/gas / diesel	Benzin [ben-'tseen]/Diesel ['dee-zel]
breakdown/repair shop	Panne ['pan-e]/Werkstatt ['verk-shtat]

FOOD & DRINK

Could you please book a table for tonight for four?	Reservieren Sie uns bitte für heute Abend einen Tisch für vier Personen [rez-er-'vee-ren zee uns 'bi-te für 'hoy-te 'aa-bent 'ein-en tish für feer pair-'zo-nen]
The menu, please	Die Speisekarte, bitte [dee 'shpei-ze-kaa-te 'bi-te]
Could I please have ...?	Könnte ich ... haben? ['kern-te ikh ... 'haa-ben]
with/without ice/ sparkling	mit [mit]/ohne Eis ['oh-ne eis]/ Kohlensäure ['koh-len-zoy-re]
vegetarian/allergy	Vegetarier(in) [veg-e-'taa-ree-er]/Allergie [al-air-'gee]
May I have the bill, please?	Ich möchte zahlen, bitte [ikh 'merkh-te 'tsaa-len 'bi-te]

SHOPPING

Where can I find...?	Wo finde ich ...? [vo 'fin-de ikh]
I'd like .../I'm looking for ...	Ich möchte ... [ikh 'merkh-te]/Ich suche ... [ikh 'zoo-khe]
pharmacy/chemist	Apotheke [a-po-'tay-ke]/Drogerie [dro-ge-'ree]
shopping centre	Einkaufszentrum [ein-kowfs-'tsen-trum]
expensive/cheap/price	teuer ['toy-er]/billig ['bil-ig]/Preis [preis]
more/less	mehr [mayr]/weniger ['vay-ni-ger]
organically grown	aus biologischem Anbau [ows bee-o-'lo-gish-em 'an-bow]

ACCOMMODATION

I have booked a room	Ich habe ein Zimmer reserviert [ikh 'haa-be ein 'tsi-me rez-erv-'eert]
Do you have any ... left?	Haben Sie noch ein ... ['haa-ben zee nokh]
single room	Einzelzimmer ['ein-tsel-tsi-mer]
double room	Doppelzimmer ['dop-el-tsi-mer]
breakfast/half board	Frühstück ['frü-shtük]/Halbpension ['halp-pen-si-ohn]
full board	Vollpension ['foll-pen-si-ohn]
shower/sit-down bath	Dusche ['doo-she]/Bad [baat]
balcony/terrasse	Balkon [bal-'kohn]/Terrasse [te-'rass-e]
key/room card	Schlüssel ['shlü-sel]/Zimmerkarte ['tsi-mer-kaa-te]
luggage/suitcase	Gepäck [ge-'pek]/Koffer ['koff-er]/Tasche ['ta-she]

BANKS, MONEY & CREDIT CARDS

bank/ATM	Bank/Geldautomat [bank/'gelt-ow-to-maat]
pin code	Geheimzahl [ge-'heim-tsaal]
I'd like to change ...	Ich möchte ... wechseln [ikh 'merkh-te ... 'vek-seln]

cash/credit card	bar [bar]/Kreditkarte [kre-'dit-kaa-te]
bill/coin	Banknote ['bank-noh-te]/Münze ['mün-tse]

HEALTH

doctor/dentist/ paediatrician	Arzt [aatst]/Zahnarzt ['tsaan-aatst]/ Kinderarzt ['kin-der-aatst]
hospital/ emergency clinic	Krankenhaus ['kran-ken-hows]/ Notfallpraxis ['note-fal-prak-sis]
fever/pain	Fieber ['fee-ber]/Schmerzen ['shmer-tsen]
diarrhoea/nausea	Durchfall ['doorkh-fal]/Übelkeit ['ü-bel-keit]
inflamed/injured	entzündet [ent-'tsün-det]/verletzt [fer-'letst]
prescription	Rezept [re-'tsept]
pain reliever/tablet	Schmerzmittel ['shmerts-mit-el]/Tablette [ta-'blet-e]

POST, TELECOMMUNICATIONS & MEDIA

stamp/letter	Briefmarke ['brief-maa-ke]/Brief [brief]
postcard	Postkarte ['posst-kaa-te]
I'm looking for a prepaid card for my mobile	Ich suche eine Prepaid-Karte für mein Handy [ikh 'zoo-khe 'ei-ne 'pre-paid-kaa-te für mein 'hen-dee]
Do I need a special area code?	Brauche ich eine spezielle Vorwahl? ['brow-khe ikh 'ei-ne shpets-ee-'ell-e 'fore-vaal]
Where can I find internet access?	Wo finde ich einen Internetzugang? [vo 'fin-de ikh 'ei-nen 'in-ter-net-tsoo-gang]
socket/adapter/ charger/wi-fi	Steckdose ['shtek-doh-ze]/Adapter [a-'dap-te]/ Ladegerät ['laa-de-ge-rayt]/WLAN ['vay-laan]

LEISURE, SPORTS & BEACH

bike/scooter rental	Fahrrad-['faa-raat]/Mofa-Verleih ['mo-fa fer-lei]
rental shop	Vermietladen [fer-'meet-laa-den]
lesson	Übungsstunde ['ü-bungs-shtun-de]

NUMBERS

0 null [null]	10 zehn [tsayn]	20 zwanzig ['tsvantsikh]
1 eins [eins]	11 elf [elf]	50 Fünfzig ['fünf-tsikh]
2 zwei [tsvei]	12 zwölf [tsvölf]	100 (ein) Hundert ['hun-dert]
3 drei [drei]	13 dreizehn [' dreitsayn]	200 Zwei Hundert [tsvei 'hun-dert]
4 vier [feer]	14 vierzehn ['feertsayn]	1000 (ein) Tausend ['tow-zent]
5 fünf [fünf]	15 fünfzehn ['fünftsayn]	2000 Zwei Tausend [tsvei 'tow-zent]
6 sechs [zex]	16 sechzehn ['zekhtsayn]	10 000 Zehn Tausend [tsayn 'tow-zent]
7 sieben ['zeeben]	17 siebzehn ['zeebtsayn]	
8 acht [akht]	18 achtzehn ['akhtsayn]	½ ein halb [ein halp]
9 neun [noyn]	19 neunzehn ['noyntsayn]	¼ ein viertel [ein 'feer-tel]

NOTES

MARCO POLO TRAVEL GUIDES

ALGARVE
AMSTERDAM
ANDALUCÍA
ATHENS
AUSTRALIA
AUSTRIA
BANGKOK
BARCELONA
BERLIN
BRAZIL
BRUGES, GHENT &
  ANTWERP
BRUSSELS
BUDAPEST
BULGARIA
CALIFORNIA
CAMBODIA
CANADA EAST
CANADA WEST
  ROCKIES
CAPE TOWN
  WINE LANDS,
  GARDEN ROUTE
CAPE VERDE
CHANNEL ISLANDS
CHICAGO
  & THE LAKES
CHINA
COLOGNE
COPENHAGEN
CORFU
COSTA BLANCA
  VALENCIA
COSTA BRAVA
  BARCELONA
COSTA DEL SOL
  GRANADA
CRETE
CUBA
CYPRUS
  NORTH AND
  SOUTH
DRESDEN
DUBAI
DUBLIN
DUBROVNIK &
  DALMATIAN COAST
EDINBURGH

EGYPT
EGYPT'S RED
  SEA RESORTS
FINLAND
FLORENCE
FLORIDA
FRENCH ATLANTIC
  COAST
FRENCH RIVIERA
  NICE, CANNES &
  MONACO
FUERTEVENTURA
GRAN CANARIA
GREECE
HAMBURG
HONG KONG
  MACAU
ICELAND
INDIA
INDIA SOUTH
  GOA & KERALA
IRELAND
ISRAEL
ISTANBUL
ITALY
JORDAN
KOS
KRAKOW
LAKE GARDA

LANZAROTE
LAS VEGAS
LISBON
LONDON
LOS ANGELES
MADEIRA
  PORTO SANTO
MADRID
MALLORCA
MALTA
  GOZO
MAURITIUS
MENORCA
MILAN
MONTENEGRO
MOROCCO
MUNICH
NAPLES &
  THE AMALFI COAST
NEW YORK
NEW ZEALAND
NORWAY
OSLO
PARIS
PHUKET
PORTUGAL
PRAGUE

RHODES
ROME
SAN FRANCISCO
SARDINIA
SCOTLAND
SEYCHELLES
SHANGHAI
SICILY
SINGAPORE
SOUTH AFRICA
STOCKHOLM
SWITZERLAND
TENERIFE
THAILAND
TURKEY
TURKEY
  SOUTH COAST
TUSCANY
UNITED ARAB
  EMIRATES
USA SOUTHWEST
VENICE
VIENNA
VIETNAM
ZÁKYNTHOS

- PACKED WITH INSIDER TIPS
- BEST WALKS AND TOURS
- FULL-COLOUR PULL-OUT MAP
  AND STREET ATLAS

STREET ATLAS

The green line ▬ indicates the Walking tours (p. 100–105)

All tours are also marked on the pull-out map

Photo: Upper Belvedere

Exploring Vienna

The map on the back cover shows how the area has been sub-divided

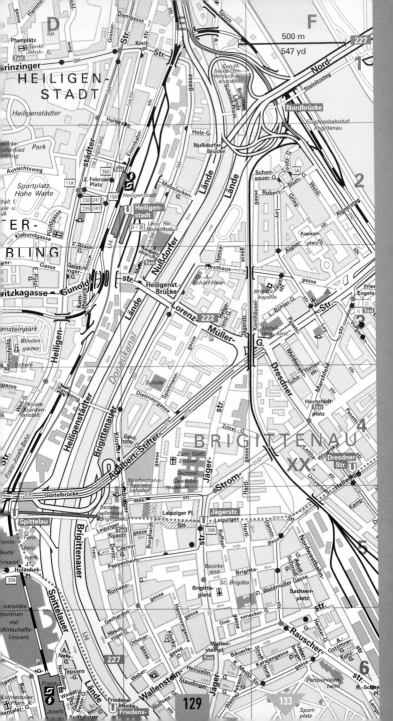

500 m
547 yd
227

1

Pfarrplatz
Sankt-Jakob- Ki.
rinzinger

HEILIGEN-
STADT

Heiligenstädter

Nordbrücke
Frachtenbahnhof
Brigittenau

ezirks-
allenbad
obling
Park

Aussichtsweg

Sportplatz
Hohe Warte

12. Februar
Platz

Holz-G.

Nußdorfer
Brücke

Schon-
gauer-G.

5A

Blum-

Wehli-

Robert-

2

Heiligenstadt

Heiligen-
stadt
P+R
Univ. für
Bodenkultur

Mooslacken-
gasse

Kapaun-
platz

ER-
BLING

Klabundgasse

Gasse

F.-Braun-

Geist-
inger-

Bosch-

Nußdorfer

Raußen-
strauch-

Taxi

Forsthaus-
Dr. A.
Schärf-Heim

Brigitta-
kapelle

Aignet-

Str.

Fried.
Engels-

2 33
N Taxi
Vo gan

3

itzkagasse

Gunold-

Heiligenst.-
Brücke

Lorenz-
222
Müller-

Heigo-
land-G.

Unfall-
Vers.-Anst.

str.

msteinpark
Blinden-
garten
Schule

Heiligenstädter

Donaukanal

Lände

Schule

Spitelmann-

Dietmayrgasse

Dresdner-

Hochstädt-
Taxi
platz

gasse

Private
Kranken-
anstalt

Rußberg

Brigittenauer

Kloster-

Adalbert-Stifter-

Zum Göttl
Erlöser
Technol.
Gewerbe-
museum

BRIGITTENAU
XX.

Dresdner
Str. U

4

Franz-Josefs-Bahn

Gürtelbrücke

Straßenbahn-
betriebs-
bahnhof

Wex-

Jager-

Strom-

Universität

Hellw

Kamp-

Spittelau

Bezirks-
hallenbad
Brigittenau

Leipziger Pl.

Jägerstr.

5

amts-
aude
ersamt
J.-
Holaubek-
Pl.

35A

Fern-
heiz-
werk

Leipziger
Spaun-

Czerny-

Pappenheim-

Burghardt-

39A

Leipziger

Raffael-

Demm-

Nordwestbahn

Brigittenauer

Spittelauer

iversitäts-
zentrum
mit
Wirtschafts-
Univers.

Romano-

Gerhardus-

Hirsch-
vogel-

Othmar-

Klucky-

Bezirks-
amt
St. Brigitta

Brigitta-
platz

Brigitta

Waldmüller Gasse

Sachsen-
platz

Wallenstein-

Hannovergasse

Grei-

senecker- G.

Rauscher-

6

227

Tepsern-
G.

Franz-

Bad-
Lichtentaler
Pfarr.
zentaler- G.

Nehr-
G.

Weber-

Heinzelm-

Wolfgang-

Staudinger-

Wasser-
G.

Friedens-
brücke
Friedens-

Jäger-

Wallenstein-

Wiesner-

Petrasch-

K.-Meißl-Str.

Karajangasse

Streffleur-

Pöchlarn-

Jäger-

Hasler-G.

Gstöttner-

Kunz-

R.-Schne-
Pl.

Pensionisten-
heim

Sportplatz

129

133

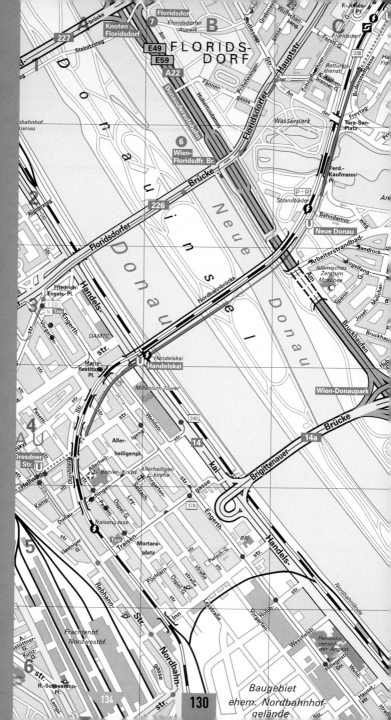

Floridsdorf 7
Floridsdorfer
Aupark

B

Knoten
Floridsdorf

227

E49
E59
A22

FLORIDS-
DORF

Stelnitzsteg

F.-Jonas-
Pl.

C

Floridsdorf
Tenstl-G.

33B

Rettungs-
dienst
Aschen-
brenner-G.

Wasserpark

Tora-San-
Platz

Freytag-
str.

6
Wien-
Floridsdfr. Br.

226

Floridsdorfer

Brücke

Neue

Ferd.-
Kaufmann-
Pl.

P+R

Strandbäder

Bahndamm-
weg

U
Neue Donau

Friedrich-
Engels-Pl.

2 33

N Taxi

Engerth-

Handels-

Donau

Arbeiterstrandbad-

Islamisches
Zentrum
Moschee

Sandrock-

Kugelfang-

str.

OAMTC

Nordbahnbrücke

insel

Spann-

Josef-

str.

Maria-
Restitun-
Pl.

U Handelskai
Handelskai

Millenium Tower

Wien-Donaupark

Donau

4

U

Dresdner
Str. U

Hellweg

Allerheiligenpl.

Wehlistr.

240

Brücke

14a

Brigittenauer

Brücke

str.

14

kai

Aller-
heiligen-

Bohler-Krkhs

Allerheiligen-
kirche

Vorgarten-

Kamp-

Donau-

Pasetti-

Leeb-
Ospel-G.

Leeb-
bach-

gasse

Engerth-

Traisengasse

Taxi Traisen-

str.

Mortara-
platz

Pöchlarn-

Ospel-G.

37A

Pielach-G.

BFI

str.

Handels-

5

Gasteiger-
G.

Rebhann

Str.

Inn

Ospel-G.

Lorystraße

Vorgarten-

Hobiln-

str.

Nordbahnlände

A.-
Stöttner-
G.

Kunz-

Frachtenbf.
Nordwestbf.

Nordbahn-

gasse

Webschel-

Pensions-
versich. der
der Angest.

Hillegeist-

Wehli-

6 str.

R.-Schneerson-
Pl.

Lampl-

134

130

Baugebiet
ehem. Nordbahnhof-
gelände

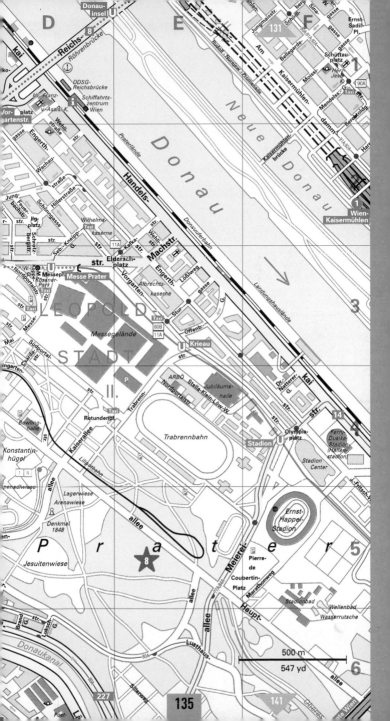

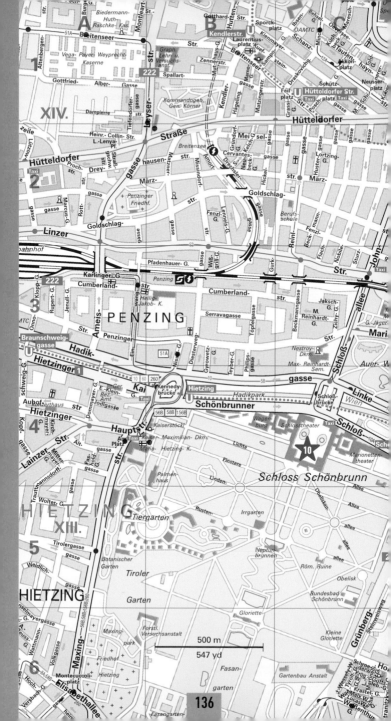

This index lists a selection of the streets and squares shown in the street atlas

KEY TO STREET ATLAS

Motorway (Freeway) Autobahn		Autoroute Autostrada
Road with four lanes Vierspurige Straße		Route à quatre voies Strada a quattro corsie
Federal / trunk road Bundes-/ Fernstraße		Route fédérale / nationale Strada statale / di grande comunicazione
Main road Hauptstraße		Route principale Strada principale
Pedestrian zone - One way road Fußgängerzone - Einbahnstraße		Zone piétonne - Rue à sens unique Zona pedonale - Via a senso unico
Railway with station Eisenbahn mit Bahnhof		Chemin de fer avec gare Ferrovia con stazione
Underground (railway) U-Bahn		Métro Metropolitana
Bus-route - Tramway Buslinie - Straßenbahn		Ligne d'autocar - Tram Linea d'autobus - Tram
Information - Youth hostel Information - Jugendherberge		Information - Auberge de jeunesse Informazioni - Ostello della gioventù
Church - Church of interest Kirche - Sehenswerte Kirche		Église - Église remarquable Chiesa - Chiesa di notevole interesse
Synagogue - Mosque Synagoge - Moschee		Synagogue - Mosquée Sinagoga - Moschea
Police station - Post office Polizeistation - Postamt		Poste de police - Bureau de poste Posto di polizia - Ufficio postale
Hospital Krankenhaus		Hôpital Ospedale
Monument - Radio or TV tower Denkmal - Funk- oder Fernsehturm		Monument - Tour d'antennes Monumento - Pilone radio o TV
Theatre - Taxi rank Theater - Taxistand		Théâtre - Station taxi Teatro - Posteggio di tassí
Fire station - School Feuerwache - Schule		Poste de pompiers - École Guardia del fuoco - Scuola
Open air -/ Indoor swimming pool Freibad - Hallenbad		Piscine en plein air - Piscine couverte Piscina all'aperto - Piscina coperta
Public toilet - Restaurant Öffentliche Toilette - Ausflugslokal		Toilette publique - Restaurant Gabinetto pubblico - Ristorante
Indoor car park - Car park Parkhaus - Parkplatz		Parking couvert - Parking Autosilo - Area di parcheggio
Walking tours Stadtspaziergänge		Promenades en ville Passeggiate urbane
MARCO POLO Highlight		MARCO POLO Highlight

INDEX

This index lists all sights, museums, and destinations, plus the names of important people and key words featured in this guide. Numbers in bold indicate a main entry.

WRITE TO US

e-mail: info@marcopologuides.co.uk

Did you have a great holiday?
Is there something on your mind?
Whatever it is, let us know!
Whether you want to praise, alert us
to errors or give us a personal tip –
MARCO POLO would be pleased to
hear from you.
We do everything we can to provide the
very latest information for your trip.

Nevertheless, despite all of our authors'
thorough research, errors can creep in.
MARCO POLO does not accept any
liability for this. Please contact us by
e-mail or post.

MARCO POLO Travel Publishing Ltd
Pinewood, Chineham Business Park
Crockford Lane, Chineham
Basingstoke, Hampshire RG24 8AL
United Kingdom

PICTURE CREDITS
Cover photograph: Hofburg with Michaelertor and fiacre (Laif: Hänel)
Biosphärenpark Wienerwald: Diry (17 top); Designpfad: Bonanza (16 top); W. Dieterich (2 centre top, 2 centre bottom, 3 top, 7, 12, 15, 26/27, 33, 40/41, 42, 45, 53, 59, 64, 67, 68 left, 72/73, 78, 89, 100/101, 106, 110 top, 110 bottom); DuMont Bildarchiv: Krause (108, 109), Wrba (4, 6, 23, 24 left, 61, 68 right, 74, 77, 111, 121); R. Freyer (34, 54); R. Hackenberg (front flap right, 3 centre, 8, 37, 48, 80/81, 82, 86, 92, 97, 108/109); Hotel Wombat's (99); Huber: Damm (25), Schmid (9); Laif: Hänel (1 top, 20), Heuer (3 bottom, 90/91), Rigaud (95, 104/105), Steinhilber (102), Stukhard (2 bottom, 24 right, 62/63); Laif/Le Figaro Magazine: Martin (84/85); Look: age fotostock (18/19), Eisenberger (106/107); mauritius images: AGE (10/11, 149), Alamy (46), allOver (56), Bernhaut (44), de Kord (front flap left), Matassa (115); Rave Up: Christian König (16 bottom); Samstag Moser & Holzinger OG: Josef Weiland (17 bottom); T. Stankiewcz (71, 107); tea-licious / Susanne Dreier-Phan Quoc: Pinie Wang (16 centre); W. M. Weiss (1 bottom); E. Wrba (2 top, 5, 38, 50)

1st Edition 2013
Worldwide Distribution: Marco Polo Travel Publishing Ltd, Pinewood, Chineham Business Park, Crockford Lane, Basingstoke, Hampshire RG24 8AL, United Kingdom. Email: sales@marcopolouk.com
© MAIRDUMONT GmbH & Co. KG, Ostfildern
Chief editor: Marion Zorn
Author: Walter Weiss, editor: Karin Liebe
Programme supervision: Ann-Katrin Kutzner, Nikolai Michaelis, Silwen Randebrock
Picture editors: Gabriele Forst, Barbara Schmid
What's hot: wunder media, Munich
Cartography street atlas & pull-out map: © MAIRDUMONT, Ostfildern
Design: milchhof : atelier, Berlin; Front cover, pull-out map cover, page 1: factor product munich
Translated from German by Robert Scott McInnes; editor of the English edition: Christopher Wynne
Prepress: M. Feuerstein, Wigel
Phrase book in cooperation with Ernst Klett Sprachen GmbH, Stuttgart, Editorial by Pons Wörterbücher

DOS & DON'TS ✊

A few tips to make your stay more enjoyable

BE GENEROUS

Tipping can also be seen under the principle of 'live and let live'. Waiters, taxi drivers, hairdressers, petrol pump attendants and lavatory attendants really rely on tips to make ends meet.

DON'T DRIVE EVERYWHERE YOURSELF OR PARK ILLEGALLY

Traffic jams and limited parking space are also notorious problems in Vienna, especially in the city centre. Do use the carparks. Most of the main sights are within walking distance of each other and there is a dense network of public transport. The EU makes it possible to collect fines even after you have left the country. If you park your car where it obstructs traffic, you will find it again – with many others – at a collecting point on the outskirts of the city and the 'parking fee' there is 170 euros. Parking offenders who are caught in the act get off cheaper if they pay their fine immediately and don't wait until they receive a summons when they return home.

MAKE SURE YOU 'PAY AND DISPLAY'

More than half the districts in Vienna are fundamentally short-stay parking zones. This is indicated by traffic signs or blue marks on the ground and parking is limited to two hours. Parking tickets (60 cents–2.40 euros depending on time) are available from tobacconists and must be carefully filled in (detailed information: *www.wien.gv.at/verkehr*).

DON'T BOOK A GROUP TRIP TO A HEURIGER

If you visit one of the *Heurigen* in Grinzing with lines of coaches in front of its gate, you will miss out on the essence of this Viennese tradition; a certain amount of intimacy is required. Go to one of the others or even to another district.

DON'T ORDER 'A CUP OF COFFEE'

If you simply order 'a cup of coffee' in a traditional café, you will immediately show your ignorance even if the waiter doesn't raise an eyebrow. In Vienna you should always order *einen kleinen* or *grossen Braunen* or *Schwarzen*, a *Kapuziner, Melange,* etc. with *Schlagobers* if you prefer it with whipped cream.

DON'T BE UNDERDRESSED IN THE STATE OPERA OR CITY CENTRE

Most culturally-interested Viennese get dressed 'in keeping with the occasion' when they go out to one of the temples of the Muses. This means: no minis or t-shirts or – heaven forbid – shorts! Men should wear a jacket. There are also some daytime taboos to observe in the Old City: bare-chested men and women in bikini tops! It is even more disapproved of if tourists go into buildings – especially churches – in such a getup.